HOUSEHOLD HACKS

pil

Publications International, Ltd.

CONTENTS

INTRODUCTION

You watch in dismay as a visitor's glass of wine tips over and spills onto your freshly-vacuumed carpet. You finally have time to clean your bathroom, only to discover that you're out of toilet-bowl cleanser. You don't quite know how to deal with a musty-smelling closet, but you do know it's just going to get worse if you don't do something.

We've all been there. *Household Hacks* includes hundreds of hacks to help you clean and maintain your home, cheaply and effectively. You'll find tips for stain removal when something gets spilled on carpet or clothing, guides for using everyday pantry products like vinegar, baking soda, and lemon juice as inexpensive cleaning solutions, and organizational tips that will make it easier to keep things neat and tidy. Learn how to keep your knickknacks polished and shiny, your upholstery fresh, and your kitchen and your bathroom odor-free.

Between long hours at work, family commitments, hobbies, and time spent with friends, we're kept busy pretty much all day, every day. It's easy to neglect our home while dust, clutter, and dirt accumulate. Cleaning and maintaining our household, though, helps make it in a soothing refuge when we need it most. This book will teach you ways to spend less time, less energy, and less money on your household tasks. ✳

CLEANING STRATEGIES

MAKE IT ROUTINE

Even people who aren't ordinarily procrastinators can find it easy to put off household tasks while they pile up. Then one day we look around, and the work seems almost insurmountable, leading us to put it off for just one more day!

By cleaning a little bit each day, and making that habit a part of your daily routine, you can make the task of household maintenance less daunting.

Your cleaning schedule for both regular and seasonal care should be organized in a way that makes you comfortable: You may choose to clean for an hour every morning, two hours after work, or all Saturday morning. As long as you have a schedule that leaves room for spontaneity, you'll stay ahead of housework.

Basic day-to-day chores, such as beds, dishes, baths, laundry, and floor care, require a firm routine. Big tasks, such as closets, ovens, and silver, are often best tackled on impulse and require an elastic plan. If a big chore is hanging over your head and you keep putting it off, wait. It will be there when you are up to it, and you'll probably do a better job if you are ready to tackle it. Remember that when you are in the mood to clean, your cleaning tasks will get done much faster if there are no interruptions.

A GENERAL PLAN

Here is a general plan for cleaning a home. We hope you'll use it as a starting point for making your own cleaning strategy.

EVERY DAY

* Remove litter from carpets and hard-surface floors.
* Wash dishes and wipe countertops and cooking appliances.
* Empty kitchen garbage containers.
* Wipe basins and bathtubs.
* Make beds and straighten rooms.

AS NEEDED

* Vacuum carpets and hard-surface floors thoroughly.
* Vacuum upholstery and drapes with the upholstery tool and use the crevice tool in the seams of furniture coverings.
* Dust and/or polish furniture.
* Clean the range and wipe out the refrigerator.
* Wash kitchen and bathroom floors.
* Clean toilets, fixtures, and bathroom mirrors.
* Change bed linens.
* Empty wastepaper baskets.

SEASONAL

* Surface-clean rugs and carpets, using a carpet-cleaning solution or an absorbent powder.
* Remove old wax, apply new wax, and buff hard-surface floors.
* Wash throw rugs.
* Shampoo upholstered furniture.
* Wash lamp shades, walls, and woodwork.
* Dust books, pictures, and lamps.

* Clean mirrors, TVs, picture frames, and art objects.
* Clean ovens, microwave, refrigerator, freezer, and other appliances.
* Wash bathroom carpeting and shower curtain.
* Organize closets.
* Turn mattresses, wash pads and pillow covers, and air or wash pillows.
* Clean screens and wash windows.

YEARLY
* Vacuum rug pads and the backs of rugs.
* Shampoo carpets, clean rugs, and turn rugs to equalize wear.
* Wash curtains, blinds, and shades, and clean draperies.
* Clean closets and cabinets.
* Wash or dry-clean bedspreads, blankets, and slipcovers.
* Clean out the garage, basement, and workshop.

IN A RUSH

The phone rings; it's a friend from school in town for a meeting or one of your mother's cousins who happens to be in the neighborhood. The surprise visitor will be at your door in 10 minutes, and your home must be ready to go on show. The following whirlwind routine will help you present a neat facade:

* Gather everything that is sitting where it doesn't belong in the entry and living areas, and dump it all into an empty laundry basket. Hide the filled basket in a closet.
* Stack newspapers and magazines on the coffee table or floor, and plump the furniture pillows.
* Give the bathroom sink and toilet a once-over, and straighten the rug and towels. Shine the mirror with tissue, and shove scattered items back into the medicine cabinet.
* Rinse the dishes, and stack them neatly in the kitchen sink or put them in the dishwasher. Wipe the countertops.
* Close the doors to rooms you don't want to display.
* Try to relax.

CLEAN A ROOM QUICKLY

Before you start to clean a room, face the fact of dirt. Cleaning is dirty work and your clothes will get soiled, so dress the part. Pull on a pair of old jeans, roll up the sleeves on a tattered shirt, and attack the grime with your full attention.

Gather together all the cleaning supplies you will need. Carrying them in a tote basket will save extra steps between your cleaning closet and your work site. Then, take everything out of the room that does not belong in it. Put small decorative items into a basket and out of harm's way, and put the dirty items that you want to clean separately, such as figurines and metal objects that need polishing, in a box or basket and take them to the kitchen.

Pull all the furniture out from the walls. Turn back rugs at the edges, and take up small scatter rugs to make vacuuming the floor easier. Choose a starting point and work your way around the room. The law of gravity applies: Dust settles downward, so to avoid dirtying what you have just cleaned, always work from the top down. Clean floors last.

With the appropriate attachment on your vacuum cleaner, dust moldings, door frames, draperies, lamp shades, blinds, shutters, pictures, wall hangings, mantels, shelves, vents, radiators, and baseboards. Vacuum upholstered furniture, as well as wood, plastic, and chrome furniture. Wipe smudges off doorknobs, light switches, and walls with an all-purpose cleaner.

Hard-surface floors are next. Using the floor-brush attachment on your vacuum cleaner, thoroughly vacuum all hard-surface flooring, such as tile, linoleum, vinyl, and wood. Now straighten the rugs that were folded back for cleaning, and vacuum them slowly. Fluff up the carpet pile.

That's it. Simply replace the furniture, dust your bric-a-brac and replace it, and your room is clean. You don't have to polish the wood furniture, wash the windows, or scrub the floors; save these special tasks for another time. It is more efficient.

Here are some quick tips to make this easy method for cleaning a room even easier:

* Carry two buckets or a bucket with two compartments when you are washing items that also need rinsing.
* Vacuum before cleaning with a liquid cleaning solution to avoid making mud.
* Go easy on cleaners. Soap or wax used sparingly clean and beautify surfaces. Use too much, and you will have to spend time removing the buildup and streaks.
* When you are cleaning something up high, don't stand on tiptoe: Grab a stepladder. If you are cleaning down low, sit on the floor. Straining up or down is tiring, inefficient, and bad for your back.

TOOLS OF THE TRADE

A well-stocked cleaning center is the hurried housecleaner's best friend. You will be more likely to start your cleaning chores and to finish the task if you have everything you need on hand and in one place. A cleaning closet will save you time and steps; it is the efficient beginning to all the quick and easy cleaning methods in this book. You may not need everything that's listed here, but as you read this section, think about the cleaning tasks you perform regularly and stock your cleaning closet with the tools that will help you accomplish them most efficiently and quickly.

Before you supply your cleaning closet, make sure the closet has a place to store all the cleaning tools and products you buy. If you can't fit them all into one orderly place, you'll waste time digging around under the sink for the cleanser and going out to the garage for your mop. Put up pegboard or hooks to hang brushes and mops. They'll not only be easier to lay your hands on, but they'll last longer if they are hung. Install plenty of shelves to hold bottles and cartons. This will get dangerous cleaning products out of the reach of children and give you space to store a full battery of cleaning supplies, so that when you find time to clean, everything you need will be handy.

* Baskets are used for carrying supplies from one room to another and for collecting dishes you want to take to the kitchen to wash, the collectibles you want to polish, and/or the toys the kids left in the family room.
* Brushes are available in an assortment of sizes: a hard-bristled scrub brush, toilet brushes (one for each bathroom), a radiator brush, and other soft- and medium-bristled brushes for scrubbing and dusting.

＊ Buckets with double compartments hold both your cleaning solution and rinse water.

＊ Cleaning cloths are made from worn-out clothes, sheets, and towels. Cotton or linen, white or light-colored fabrics are best.

＊ Mops should have detachable heads for easy cleaning.

＊ Rubber gloves only protect your hands if you wear them. Don't forget to put yours on whenever you work with cleaning solutions. Scouring pads are made of both synthetics and steel wool. Keep a variety in your cleaning closet. Sponges should be tossed out as soon as they start to shred. Have plenty on hand.

＊ Stepladders, at least three feet tall, are a safe substitute for the unsteady chair.

＊ Your vacuum cleaner with a set of cleaning tools and a small handheld vacuum are some of the most essential tools in your cleaning closet.

＊ A balled-up pair of pantyhose can serve as a nonscratch pad to scrub walls, windows, sinks, and bathtubs.

＊ If you run out of paper towels, coffee filters can fill in and help mop up spills.

＊ Old toothbrushes work well to clean combs, silverware, and tile grout.

CLEANING YOUR CLEANING TOOLS

When you clean, your cleaning tools absorb all that dirt and grime. Ironically, you need to clean your cleaners!

✳ Clean and deodorize smelly floor mops or sponges by soaking them for 10 minutes in a gallon of water mixed with 3/4 cup bleach. Rinse thoroughly afterward.

✳ Eliminate residue and smells from mops or rags by soaking them in a mixture of 4 tablespoons baking soda and 1 gallon water.

✳ Soak a well-worn, smelly sponge in a shallow dish of vinegar for several hours. Rinse sponge well, then let dry. In humid weather, store the sponge in a shallow dish of vinegar to keep it from souring.

CLEANING AGENTS

In addition to your cleaning tools, you need to have on hand several basic cleaning supplies. Keep in mind that products that are tough on grime are often tough on you, especially your hands, face, and lungs. Always read product labels. When cleaning with bleach, ammonia, or borax, wear rubber gloves and keep the area well ventilated. Also, don't mix bleach with ammonia—it can produce a poisonous gas.

✳ **All-purpose cleaners** remove grease and grimy dirt.

✳ **Ammonia** is available in clear or sudsy form. It is an excellent cleaner or cleaning booster for many household surfaces. It is a grease cutter, wax stripper, window cleaner, and general soil remover. If you object to the strong odor of ammonia, buy a scented product, but neither scented ammonia nor sudsy ammonia is suitable for stain removal.

* **Baking soda** is one of the most versatile cleaning products available. Used by itself in dry form, it acts as a very mild scouring powder that will not scratch even the most delicate surfaces. Add water to make a paste, and use baking soda to scour dirty surfaces. Combined with other ingredients, it makes a very good cleaning solution that also deodorizes.
* **Baking powder** can be used to remove odors, among other applications.
* **Bleach** helps remove stains and whiten laundry, and it's also good for cleaning toilets.
* **Flour** is useful for some cleaning tasks. Always use flour in its dry form because it creates a gluey paste when mixed with water.
* **Lemon juice,** either bottled or squeezed from a cut lemon, provides the mild acid reaction needed for many cleaning solutions.
* **Liquid dishwashing detergents** can be used for many cleaning tasks in addition to doing dishes.
* **Salt** is surprisingly versatile in helping clean, prevent messes, and remove odors.
* **Vinegar** is also an acid; it can usually be substituted for lemon juice. White vinegar should be used to clean fabrics, but cider vinegar is adequate for most other applications.
* **Waxes, polishes, and oils** shine and protect wood, leather, brass, chrome, silver, glass, and other surfaces.

Throughout this book, we'll provide many homemade cleaning solutions. Some will be colorless. It's essential that you clearly label each bottle, but you can also let food coloring identify at least one at a glance. For example, put a few drops of blue food color in the window cleaner spray bottle.

TIPS WHILE YOU CLEAN

* Don't let those unreachable cobwebs way up there get you down. Wrap a tennis ball in a dust rag; secure it with a few rubber bands. Assuming the room is free of breakables, toss the ball at the webs.

* If you're planning to wear rubber gloves for any cleaning task, first pour a little cornstarch into your palm and rub your hands together to make the gloves easier to slide on.

* Sprinkling baking powder into rubber gloves is another way to ensure they'll come right off when your work is done.

* Put a rubber band around each spray bottle and other cleaning-product containers. Tuck a sponge or clean cloth under the band so you'll always have one at hand.

* **Windows:** Wipe horizontally on the outside and vertically on the inside, so you'll know on which side of the glass any streaks lie. Choose a cloudy day rather than a sunny one for cleaning windows: The sun dries the glass too quickly and causes streaks.

* **Walls:** Wash painted walls from the top to the bottom. This prevents water from dripping down the wall, creating hard-to-remove streaks.

* **Dusting and Vacuuming:** Clean a room by first dusting its highest surface and then working your way down. With gravity's help, dust and dirt settle down to the floor. Vacuum or sweep the floor last.

* Are your hands a mess from grease, gardening, or generally getting things done? Clean very dirty hands by scrubbing with cornmeal that has been moistened with a little bit of apple cider vinegar. Thoroughly scrub your hands. Rinse well and dry; repeat if necessary. Your hands will be soft and smooth—and the dirt will be gone!

Many of our ancestors hid their kitchens in their basements or backyards or off in some far, dark corner of the house. That was one way to keep the family from knowing you hadn't gotten around to cleaning the oven for a few years. Today, most of us have a different attitude about kitchens. We want our kitchens to be light, sparkling (or cozy) multiuse family centers, complete with computers and couches, TVs, and miniature vegetable patches.

Gathering the family around the hearth or the induction cooktop is a terrific idea. But don't forget that in the middle of all the activity and nice furniture, there's still a kitchen, where you're going to be spilling milk and burning toast.

Cooking is a messy task: You can't make an omelet without breaking eggs, dripping egg white down the outside of the bowl onto the counter, or dropping a shell on the floor and stepping on it. The only way to deal with the mess in the kitchen is to control it with quick, daily cleanups.

In most households, there are cooks and there are eaters. Use this division of labor to everyone's advantage for regular kitchen maintenance. Cooks are responsible for blotting spills when they happen and getting dirty cooking utensils into the sink or dishwasher. But after dinner, the cleanup crew takes over from the cooks. Keeping the kitchen fairly clean beats having to spend regular long stretches of time cleaning it. We have dozens of hacks to help you keep your kitchen clean, sanitary, and organized.

Try this recipe for a basic everyday cleanser in your kitchen:

¼ cup vinegar
1 squirt Dawn dishwashing liquid
Enough water to fill a 32-ounce bottle
5 drops peppermint oil or any essential oil (for fragrance)

It won't tackle the tough, greasy jobs, but using this cleanser daily can help control grease buildup, remove spills, and keep your kitchen smelling nice. In fact, you can customize the essential oil fragrance to suit your taste. (The oil is only for fragrance and will not affect the cleaning ability of this solution.)

Keep the solution in a spray bottle, and make sure you clearly label its contents. Shake well before each use. Spray on countertops and appliances, then wipe off with a damp cloth or sponge.

COUNTERTOPS

Kitchen countertops have to be ready for anything—a smack from a floury handful of bread dough, a slice from a paring knife that goes off course, or a slosh of grape juice intent on staining the surface. Acrylic, ceramic tile, cultured marble, marble, plastic laminate, and wood countertops can take this kind of abuse if we make it up to them with regular, gentle cleaning and care. These surfaces are all easy to clean; if they can't take it, they should get out of the kitchen.

TIPS WHILE YOU CLEAN

* Remove stains from laminate countertops with a paste of baking soda and water. Apply, let dry, then rub off and rinse.

* Use club soda to clean your kitchen counters, stovetop, and stainless-steel fixtures. Just pour it directly on a sponge and wipe clean. Rinse with warm water, then dry thoroughly.

* Wipe your kitchen countertops with undiluted distilled white vinegar once a day to shine them and keep your kitchen smelling fresh.

* Rub a piece of wax paper over your tile or laminate kitchen countertops. The shine will send you reaching for your sunglasses.

* Remove permanent marker from countertops and appliances with isopropyl rubbing alcohol.

* Clean polished marble and metal surfaces with chalk. Crush white chalk in a clear storage bag, tapping it gently with a hammer. Dip a soft cloth into the powder and rub.

* Butcher-block and other wood countertops require more care than you might expect, if you don't want them to look like they belong in the back room of a butcher shop. You can restore a wood countertop that has been scratched and stained by sanding it and applying a wood-preservative product, but that's a lot of work. You'll save time in the long run by preserving your wood countertop's good looks. Always use a cutting board on a wood countertop, just as you would with any other surface. Wipe up stains and keep your wood countertops as dry as you possibly can. Periodically, rub oil into wood countertops to protect them from moisture. Use boiled linseed oil or salad oil and follow the procedure described below.

* Remove stains with a solution of ¼ cup chlorine bleach in 1 quart warm water. Rinse, dry, and coat with oil.

* To get rid of odors, rub the surface with a slice of lemon.

CLEANER FOR ACRYLIC OR CULTURED-MARBLE

Mix ½ cup vinegar, 1 cup ammonia, and ¼ cup baking soda in 1 gallon hot water. **Caution:** Wear rubber gloves and work in a well-ventilated area when using this powerful solution. Apply it to the countertop with a sponge, rinse with clear water, and buff dry.

WOOD COUNTERTOP CLEANER

Baking soda cleans and deodorizes wood surfaces. Mix ½ cup baking soda in 1 quart warm water. **Caution:** Wear rubber gloves. Rub the paste into the wood countertop, using a synthetic scouring pad. Rinse well with clear water and pat dry to remove excess moisture. When completely dry, restore the finish by using boiled linseed oil or salad oil, rubbed in with a fine-grade steel-wool pad. Treat the countertop with two coats of oil, applied 24 hours apart, and blot up the excess oil after each application.

CUTTING BOARDS

✳ You can keep odors from a clean wood or plastic cutting board by wiping it with a sponge dampened with a little vinegar.

✳ After cleaning your wood cutting board, rub a bit of lemon juice on it to help get rid of garlic, onion, or fish smells.

* Use bleach to keep a wood cutting board free of bacteria. Wash the cutting board in hot, sudsy water and rinse thoroughly. Then mix 3 tablespoons bleach with 1 gallon warm water. Soak or brush the solution onto the cutting board, keep it moist for at least 2 minutes, then rinse thoroughly.

* Deodorize and remove stains from wood cutting boards, bowls, or utensils with a solution of 4 tablespoons baking soda to 1 quart water.

* To disinfect a plastic cutting board after it's been washed, place it in a solution of 1 tablespoon bleach per gallon of water. Soak for 2 minutes; drain and air-dry.

SINKS & FIXTURES

Get in the habit of wiping faucets and taps when you swab the counters after meals. This will prevent water spots and give your kitchen a sparkling look with very little effort on your part. Clean hardware when you clean the sink, using the same cleaning product and method. Rinse well and buff with a dry cloth. Wash greasy drain baskets in the dishwasher.

If you live in an area that has hard water, you'll need to remove mineral deposits from faucet heads. Remove the head from its fitting, take it apart, and soak it in vinegar. Then brush the mineral deposits loose with a toothbrush. If the holes remain clogged, poke them clear with a wire, pin, toothpick, or ice pick.

* Remove water spots from stainless-steel appliances and fixtures using a cloth dampened with isopropyl rubbing alcohol.

* Clean stainless-steel sinks with a paste of baking soda and water, or sprinkle baking soda directly onto a sponge and scrub the surface. Rinse and buff dry.

* Clean chrome fixtures by simply wiping them with plain vinegar. If the chrome is heavily spotted, wipe with a sponge dampened with vinegar and sprinkled with a little baking soda.

* Just one dryer sheet can control odor and musty smells under your bathroom or kitchen sink.

Mix lemon juice and salt to the consistency of toothpaste, and apply to brass, copper, or stainless-steel sinks and fixtures. Gently scrub, then rinse.

UNCLOGGING THE DRAIN

We all know that cooking grease combined with bits of food jams kitchen-sink drains, and we know that prevention is the best cure for the problem. But most of us will have blocked kitchen drains anyway.

As soon as a drain begins to run slowly, treat it; don't wait until no water drains out. Here are some other suggestions:

* Pour a strong salt solution of 1 cup salt and 2 cups hot water down the kitchen drain to eliminate odors and break up grease deposits.
* To dislodge greasy foods that may be clogging up your drain, sprinkle 1/2 cup salt and 1/2 cup baking soda into the drain. Run hot tap water to flush.
* Once a week, pour a can of Pepsi down the drain to keep it clear and unclogged.
* Clear kitchen sink drainpipes of mold- and bacteria-breeding food particles. Once a week, pour in a solution of 1 tablespoon bleach in 1 gallon water. Wait a few minutes, then flush with cold running water for several minutes.

Baking soda and vinegar will foam your drain clean and help prevent clogs. Pour 1/2 cup baking soda down the drain, followed by 1 cup distilled white vinegar. When foam subsides, rinse with hot water. This also works well on garbage disposals.

If these treatments do not open the drain and if either a dishwasher or a garbage disposal is connected to it, call a plumber immediately. If no appliances utilize the drain, you can attempt to open it with a plumber's helper.

If plunging fails to unclog the drain, use a chemical drain cleaner. These products must be handled with special care because they are caustic and harmful to skin and eyes. Use them in a well-ventilated area and follow the manufacturer's instructions carefully. Commercial drain openers are sold in granular, liquid, and pressurized forms. Granular products utilize lye to do their work, liquid drain openers use lye and other chemicals, and pressurized products work by chlorofluorocarbon propellants and pressure. Before you use a granular drain opener, you must remove standing water from the sink; this is not necessary for liquids.

If the first type of chemical drain opener you use does not work, do not use a different drain opener unless the initial cleaner has been flushed away totally. Never use a plunger or a pressurized drain opener after using a chemical cleaner; either one may cause dangerous chemicals to splash back onto you. Also, be sure to tell your plumber what you have put into the drain before he or she starts to work. The combination of ammonia and other household cleaners with drain cleaners produces hazardous gases.

FRIDGE & FREEZER

If you keep up appearances by regularly wiping sticky fingerprints off the refrigerator door and gummy drips off the front of the freezer, you can put off cleaning the messes that lurk within your large appliances until you have time to deal with them thoroughly.

✳ To clean and refresh the inside of your refrigerator, sprinkle equal amounts of salt and baking soda onto a damp sponge and wipe down all surfaces. Wipe clean with a fresh sponge dampened with water.

✳ Remove mildew spots and prevent mildew buildup inside your refrigerator by wiping occasionally with a sponge dampened in undiluted vinegar. A toothbrush is an excellent tool for reaching inside the folds of the rubber seals. No need to rinse afterward.

✳ Use a clean, dry toothbrush to remove crumbs and crud from the seals around refrigerator and freezer doors.

✳ Place a sheet of aluminum foil on the floor of your freezer to keep spills and ice cube trays from sticking. Be sure not to cover any vents or other openings.

✳ Trying to vacuum under the refrigerator or another hard-to-reach spot? Put a cardboard tube from a roll of paper towels, gift wrap, or another product on the end of the hose attachment. For narrow openings, bend or flatten the tube.

✳ Don't waste a ruined pair of pantyhose—use it to clean under your refrigerator. Wrap the nylon around a yardstick, then run it under the fridge.

✳ To remove any unpleasant taste in ice cubes from an automatic ice cube maker, clean the removable parts of the unit with baking soda and water.

OVEN & STOVETOP

Ovens and stovetops can be a hot mess. Here are a few tips to help.

✳ Stovetop spills can be cleaned up easily if first sprinkled with salt. The mildly abrasive quality of salt removes stuck-on food, but it won't mar your stove's surface.

✳ Clean burned-on food from a stovetop burner by sprinkling it with a mixture of salt and ground cinnamon, then wiping away immediately. The mixture will give off a pleasant smell and cover up any burnt odor the next time you turn on the burner.

* Soak up liquid spills on stovetop burners in much the same way, sprinkling with a mixture of salt and ground cinnamon. Leave mixture on spill for 5 minutes to absorb liquid, then wipe away.

* To prevent grease splatters from sticking to the wall behind your stove, spray a painted or wallpapered wall with furniture polish and buff it with a soft cloth.

* Make your oven practically self-cleaning! In a glass baking dish, mix 2 cups warm water and 1/4 cup ammonia. Place it in the oven, shut the door, and let it work overnight. The next morning, sprinkle oven with baking soda and wipe clean with a damp sponge...and no elbow grease.

* Combine equal parts vinegar and hot water in a small bowl. Use this solution and a sponge to rub away any dried-on stains in your oven and help prevent grease buildup.

* Eliminate the odor from a commercial oven cleaner with a solution of 2 cups vinegar and 3 quarts warm water. Dip a sponge into mixture and wring it well, then wipe down the inside surfaces of the oven. There's no need to rinse.

* If a pie or similar sugary confection boils over in your oven, sprinkle the sticky spill with salt while the oven is still hot. Let it sit until spilled area becomes crisp, then lift off with a spatula when oven cools.

* Get rid of stubborn baked-on or blackened areas on an oven rack by "steaming" off the soot with ammonia vapors. Just lay the rack on an old towel in your bathtub. (Be sure the bathroom is well ventilated.) Fill the tub with warm water and 1/2 cup ammonia; let sit for half an hour. Rinse. (This also works for barbecue grill racks.)

* A similar technique for loosening burned-on foods from oven or grill racks is to place the racks in a trash bag. Mix 1 cup baking soda and 1/2 cup ammonia and pour over the racks. Close the bag and let sit overnight. Scrub and rinse well in the morning.

* Combine the following ingredients to cut grease buildup on stoves, backsplashes, or glossy enamel surfaces: 3 cups baking soda, 2 cups vinegar, 1 cup ammonia, and 1 gallon hot water. Wear rubber gloves when you wipe on the mixture, making sure room is well ventilated. Wipe clean with a damp sponge.

* Clean up a grease spatter on the kitchen wall with a bit of cornstarch on a paper towel or soft cloth. Gently rub the grease spot until it's gone.

* To clean a hamburger grill or pancake griddle, pour brewed coffee onto the surface (the surface can be warm or cold). Wait a few minutes, then wipe clean with a soft cloth—make sure the surface has cooled before you do this.

Spills on stovetops and in ovens are no match for this mixture: Make a paste of lemon juice, water, and baking soda. Apply to spills, let sit 15 minutes, then scrub and rinse with water and a sponge.

DISHWASHER

Baking soda cleans your dishwasher inside and out. Dip a damp cloth in soda and use it to clean smudges and fingerprints from the exterior; the same method will also remove stains from the liner. Use a synthetic scouring pad to clean stubborn soil.

∗ Use a spray glass cleaner to polish chromium trim. Commercial kitchen-appliance waxes will leave a protective wax coating on your dishwasher, but be careful not to get wax on the plastic parts.

∗ Remove dried-on food or detergent from the chrome inside your dishwasher by rubbing with a piece of lemon. Wipe clean with a damp cloth, then rub dry with a clean, dry cloth.

∗ Add 1/2 cup vinegar to an empty dishwasher and run the rinse cycle. This will clear any clogs in the dishwasher drain lines and deodorize the machine.

MICROWAVE

∗ If your microwave is spattered with old sauces and greasy buildup, place a glass measuring cup with 1 cup water and 1/4 cup vinegar inside microwave. Boil for 3 minutes, then remove the measuring cup and wipe inside of oven with a damp sponge.

∗ Microwaves are veritable safe-deposit boxes for odors. Clean the inside and outside with a little baking soda on a damp sponge; rinse well. Between uses, keep an open box of baking soda in the closed microwave. Change it every 30 days.

* To remove the lingering smell of burned microwave popcorn, heat a small glass dish of pure vinegar in the microwave for 5 minutes on a low heat setting. Remove and wipe down inside of oven.

* Deodorize your microwave by keeping a dish of vinegar inside overnight. If smells persist, change vinegar and repeat procedure nightly.

COFFEE & TEAPOTS

* Buildup in a coffeemaker's brewing system can affect coffee flavor. Get rid of buildup by running a brewing cycle with cold water and 1/4 cup vinegar. Follow with a cycle of clean water. If you can still smell vinegar, run another cycle using fresh water.

* Remove coffee stains and mineral buildup from the glass pot of an automatic drip coffeemaker by adding 1 cup crushed ice, 1 tablespoon water, and 4 teaspoons salt to the pot when it is at room temperature. Gently swirl mixture, rinse, and wash as usual.

* To clean a teapot or stovetop percolator, fill it with water, add 2 or 3 tablespoons baking soda, and boil for 10 to 15 minutes. After cooling, scrub and rinse thoroughly.

* To clean the inside of a teapot, add the peel of 1 lemon per 2 cups warm water. Soak overnight.

SMELL-BUSTERS

* Garlic and onion odors on countertops respond to a solution of 1 tablespoon bleach and 1 cup water. Wash the surface, then let the solution sit for about 5 minutes. Rinse well.

* If you come home to a foul-smelling fridge full of leftovers you forgot to trash before your trip, toss the mess immediately. Clean up any excess with a sponge or a paper towel, then gather 6 or more coffee filters. Fill each filter with 1/2 cup baking soda; place 1 or more on each shelf and compartment to absorb odors quickly. Remove when odor is gone.

* Kitchen odors disappear thanks to the freshening power of lemons and a few spices. Fill a small pot with water. Add several pieces of lemon rind and about 1 teaspoon each of whole cloves and rosemary leaves. Bring to a boil. The aroma will soon reach nearly every room of your house.

* Freshen the air in your kitchen with the simplest of methods. Heat the oven to 300 degrees Fahrenheit and place a whole lemon on the center rack. With the door slightly ajar, let the lemon "cook" for about 15 minutes; turn off oven. Let lemon cool before removing it.

* Disguise burnt smells with a touch of ground cinnamon. Sprinkle a bit in a pie plate and place in a warm oven for about 10 minutes.

* Boil 1 tablespoon vinegar in 1 cup water to eliminate smoky smells in the kitchen.

* Freshen a plastic lunch box by filling it with water and 1/4 cup vinegar. Let stand for 12 hours, then rinse with fresh water.

* An open box of baking soda in the refrigerator or freezer absorbs odors for up to 3 months.

* To remove odors from a garbage disposal, cut up a lemon, toss it in, and grind it up. Oranges and limes also work to freshen the disposal.

* Remove fish, onion, or garlic odor from hands with a solution of 3 parts baking soda to 1 part water or Ivory Liquid Hand Cleanser. Rub, then rinse.

* Alternately, rub a few coffee beans in your hands; the oil released absorbs the odor. Wash your hands with soap and warm water once the odor is gone.

* To remove onion odor from your hands, sprinkle on a little salt, then moisten with a bit of vinegar. Rub hands together and rinse.

* If your hands smell like garlic, rub a cut lemon over them.

PREVENTING A MESS WHILE YOU COOK

* Ingredients such as dried fruits won't stick to a knife if you rub a bit of vegetable oil on the blade before chopping.

* Mix and dispense in 2 easy steps—no cleanup required! Mix ingredients for deviled eggs or stuffed mushrooms by placing all ingredients in a plastic food storage bag. Seal it and knead to blend contents. To dispense the mixture, snip off a small corner of the still-sealed bag. Then just squeeze and stuff! When you're done, throw away your "dispenser."

* When you need cracker crumbs for a recipe, put your crackers in a plastic food storage bag and squeeze out most of the air. Seal it almost all the way, leaving it open at the corner so air can escape. Crush crackers by rolling a rolling pin up and down the bag. This contains the mess, crushes the crackers, and keeps your rolling pin clean.

* Before you prepare food on a countertop, cover the surface with a large sheet of either wax or parchment paper. Put it under any cutting boards too. This is especially important when working with meat, chicken, or fish.

* Spread a sheet of aluminum foil on the oven rack below a baking pan if you fear boilovers and spills. (Don't spread the foil on the bottom of an oven.)

* Pots are less likely to boil over when you use this tiny tool: a tiny toothpick laid flat between the lid and the pot. The space allows just enough steam to escape to prevent boilovers. This works when baking covered casserole dishes too.

* Melt chocolate without the messy bowl or pan to wash afterward. Pour chocolate chips, squares, or pieces into a plastic food storage bag and squeeze out most of the air. Seal and place bag in a pan of warm (but not boiling) water. When the chocolate is melted, snip off a small corner of the still-sealed bag; squeeze it into a recipe or use it to decorate a cake.

* Keep that cookbook clean while you cook. Open it to the proper page, then cover it with or enclose it in a plastic food storage bag.

* Picking up the mess from a dropped egg can be tricky. Make it easier by sprinkling the mess with salt and letting stand 15 minutes. The salt absorbs and solidifies the runny egg. Wipe away with a paper towel.

* If you spill a small amount of cooking oil, sprinkle it with salt. Wipe up spill after about 15 minutes.

* Add a quick shot of cooking spray to the lip of a measuring cup or pitcher to prevent drips.

* Clearing the table after a big dinner party can be a challenge. To get a head start on doing the dishes, line a large bowl with a plastic grocery bag, handles overlapping the edges. Place it prominently in your kitchen with a rubber spatula alongside. As the plates are brought into the kitchen, scrape the scraps right into the bowl. Once the plates are clean, it's a snap to pick the bag up by the handles and toss.

* Save yourself some steps and keep your countertops neater. Line a coffee can with a small plastic bag; place it near the sink and fill it with peelings and scraps. Make just 1 trip to the kitchen trash to toss the bag when you're done rather than traipsing back and forth.

* When you can't wash the breakfast dishes immediately, sprinkle plates with salt to keep eggs from sticking and make dishes easier to clean later.

* Soft cheese or other sticky food stuck on a grater? Cut a lemon in half and rub the pulp side on both surfaces of the grater.

* Place an entire roll or coil of garbage bags in the bottom of your garbage can. When you fill up one bag, remove it and just pull up a new one.

FOOD HACKS—PREPARATION & STORAGE

* To keep hamburger patties separated in the freezer, place a plastic coffee can lid between each one. Store them all in a plastic freezer bag. When the time comes to cook them, the patties will separate easily, even when frozen.

* Cookies lift off a cookie sheet easily if you run a piece of unflavored dental floss underneath them.

* Keep dough from sticking to cookie cutters with a light application of cooking spray beforehand.

* Instead of greasing cookie sheets, line them with parchment paper. The cookies bake more evenly, they cool right on the pan, and cleanup is minimal.

* Picking silk from a freshly shucked ear of corn can be a tedious job. Speed up the process by wiping a damp paper towel across the ear; it will pick up the strands.

* Dry lettuce faster than you can say "spin cycle"! Wash the leaves and shake off as much water as you can. Place them in a plastic grocery bag lined with paper towels. Grasp the bag by the handles (or let your kids have the fun) and whirl it around in circles until the lettuce is dry.

* Slightly wilted produce can be brought back to life if you sprinkle it with cool water, wrap in a paper towel, and refrigerate for about an hour.

* Keep potatoes from sprouting by storing apples with them.

* Hard cheeses that are difficult to cut can be tamed by cutting through them with unflavored dental floss.

* Cut fruit will stay fresh in the refrigerator without turning brown if you coat it with lemon juice.

* Hold an orange under hot water for a bit before you squeeze it. You'll get twice the juice!

* Many fruits ripen more quickly and evenly at room temperature in a paper lunch bag. These include tomatoes, peaches, pears, and avocados. Wrap green bananas first in a damp dishtowel, then place in bag. When the produce is sufficiently ripened, refrigerate as usual.

* Before you stow uncut lemons in the refrigerator, put them in a jar of water. They will be juicier and will last longer than lemons stored in the produce drawer.

* If a lemon is too firm to juice, try either of these methods: Microwave it on high in 10-second increments until soft enough, or boil it for a few minutes.

* To get just a few drops of juice from a lemon or lime, pierce the whole fruit with a toothpick. Squeeze out what you need, then use the toothpick to plug the hole. Refrigerate.

* Salt can help remove gritty dirt from fresh vegetables. To wash arugula, leeks, or spinach, trim them and place in a bowl of lukewarm water. Add a tablespoon of salt, swish vegetables around, and let soak for 20 to 30 minutes. Transfer vegetables to a colander and rinse thoroughly.

* Keep a spray bottle of vinegar near your kitchen sink and use it to spritz vegetables before you rinse them with cold running water. The vinegar will help dissolve pesticide residue.

* Tomatoes are easier to peel if you place them in a heatproof bowl and cover them with boiling water. Wait 1 minute, then drain.

* Tomatoes ripen best when placed stem-side up, not touching each other, and out of direct sunlight. They may look nice on a windowsill, but that may cause soft spots.

* Freshen up fish just brought home from the market by returning it to its natural environment for a short time. Add 1 tablespoon sea salt to 2 quarts cold water, then add a lot of ice cubes. Soak fish in this salt water for about 15 minutes, then remove and dry it off before preparing as desired.

* It's easiest to marinate meats not in a bowl or pan but in a quart- or gallon-size food storage bag. The bag allows for full coverage, and you can easily flip the bag at intervals to make sure the marinade reaches all parts of the meat.

* Grind peppercorns or crush other whole spices by placing them in a snack-size food storage bag and smashing with a meat-tenderizing hammer or even a rolling pin.

* To grease a pan or cookie sheet with shortening, slip a food storage bag over your hand and dip it directly into the shortening container. Rub your hand over the pan to spread the shortening. Keep the bag in the shortening container for next time.

Test baking soda freshness by pouring a small amount of vinegar or lemon juice over 1/2 teaspoon of baking soda. If it doesn't actively bubble, it's too old to use. Alternatively, you can put a few teaspoons in a cup of water. If—right away—it fizzes, it's still good.

STORAGE & CONTAINERS

✳ When you finish a product that comes in a plastic squeeze bottle, don't toss the bottle in the recycling bin. Rinse it well and let it air-dry. These bottles are just right for storing and dispensing many of the surprising solutions found in this book.

✳ Save space and keep place mats handy by hanging them inside a pantry or cabinet door. Clip a set together with a binder clip.

✳ Group cloth napkin sets together in a drawer or hall pantry with a binder clip. When it's time to set the table for company, you'll have a full set at the ready.

✳ After the dishes are washed and you're ready to store them, insert a flattened coffee filter between china plates and saucers—or other delicate pieces—to protect them.

✳ Clean mineral deposits and neutralize any acids in old canning jars by shaking a solution of 4 tablespoons baking soda per quart of warm water inside. Rinse thoroughly, then sterilize as usual.

✳ Plasticware, especially food containers, often takes on a greasy feeling. Put a capful of bleach in the dishwater along with your usual dishwashing liquid. Problem solved!

✳ Scrub stained plastic storage containers with a paste of lemon juice and baking soda.

✳ Avoid red tomato stains on plastic by spraying a container with cooking spray before adding tomato-based food. Before washing the container, rinse with cold water.

Always check the label on boxed and canned goods to see how they should be stored. If you haven't refrigerated items that should be refrigerated, don't use them! Throw them away.

High-acid canned foods, such as tomatoes, keep for between 12 and 18 months, while low-acid foods can keep up to 5 years. To be on the safe side, try to use all canned foods within a year of purchase.

Potatoes and onions should not be refrigerated, but they do need to be kept cooler than most foods stored in cupboards. If you don't have a cellar, make sure you store them in the coolest place possible.

Don't crowd the refrigerator or freezer. Air needs to circulate to keep temperatures even.

Use home-frozen fruits and vegetables within a year.

DISHWASHER

Almost every meal you eat at home results in dirty dishes. That could be more than a thousand sinkfuls of dishes annually. Washing dishes is one of the few housecleaning tasks that is truly unavoidable; the trick is to get it done and out of the way as quickly as possible. Here are a few hints to help you do dishes without doing yourself in.

* Of course, the best hint for making dishwashing easier is to use a dishwasher. If you have a dishwasher, carefully read the manufacturer's instructions for loading, correct water temperatures, and preferred dishwasher detergents.

* Remove food residues from dinnerware as quickly as possible. Scrape dishes with a rubber scraper or plastic brush to prevent scratches. Never scrape plates with knives or other sharp objects. Rinse out coffeecups and teacups before residues have a chance to stain the cups. Use cool water to soak or wash dishes that have been used to serve

eggs or cheese. Acid foods, such as tomatoes, vinegar, and wine, allowed to remain on glazed dinnerware can pit the surface.

✳ To protect glass or china from chipping or breaking while you are hand washing it, use a plastic dishpan or rubber sink mat. You can also pad the bottom of the sink with a towel. Avoid abrupt changes of temperature when you wash china.

✳ Do not wash delicate, hand-painted, gold- or silver-trimmed, or antique dinnerware in the dishwasher. Metal-trimmed dinnerware should also not be soaked in soapy water for long periods of time; this will damage the trim.

✳ High temperatures may also damage dishes. Do not warm plates in the oven unless they are heatproof. Do not rinse glazed dinnerware with very hot or boiling water; this may cause the glaze to craze, or develop minute cracks.

GLASSWARE

Most glassware can be safely washed in the dishwasher, but gilt- and silver-trimmed glass, delicate crystal, milk glass, and ornamental glass must be washed by hand. If you have soft water in your area, we recommend that you wash all glassware by hand because the combination of soft water and dishwasher detergent will etch and permanently dull glassware.

Before you wash glassware, cushion the bottom of the sink with a towel or rubber mat. Add vinegar to the wash water or rinse water for more sparkle; ammonia in the wash water will cut grease on glassware.

Wash glasses first, before cutlery or dinnerware. Slowly slide stemware into the wash water, holding the glass by the base; if you push a glass into the water bottom first, it could crack. Remove dirt from crevices with a soft-bristled brush; remove stains by rubbing with a cut lemon or washing in a vinegar solution. Let glassware drip dry upside down, or polish with a soft, lint-free cloth.

✳ Clean stained decanters by filling them with water and adding 1 cup ammonia or vinegar. Soak overnight. If this solution does not clean the decanter, use two packs of powdered denture cleaner dissolved in water.

1886: Josephine Garis Cochran of Shelbyville, Illinois, unable to find a machine to wash dishes more efficiently than her servants, invents one. She receives patent #355,139 for the first practical dish-washing machine.

1893: Cochran introduces her dishwasher at the Chicago World's Fair; when restaurants and hotels express interest, she founds a manufacturing company that eventually becomes KitchenAid.

1926: Kohler Company introduces the Electric Sink, but it's discontinued during the Great Depression.

1949: KitchenAid introduces the KD-10, the first residential dishwasher to distribute water by a pressurized system rather than just splashing water on dishes.

* Crystal is best washed by hand, very carefully. After washing, dip crystal in a sink full of warm water and 1 tablespoon vinegar. Finish with a clear water rinse.
* Get rid of the cloudy film on glassware by soaking items overnight in a tub of equal parts vinegar and warm water. Wash glasses by hand the next day.

FLATWARE & CUTLERY

Most of us wash the knives, forks, and spoons we use at mealtimes along with our other dishes. If we're organized and wash dishes by hand, the flatware is washed after the glasses and before the plates. But washing flatware doesn't complete the cleaning process; unless you eat with stainless steel, your flatware will need to be polished occasionally.

Cutlery (knives and other cutting instruments) can be cleaned in the same way as flatware, but observe the manufacturer's instructions to be sure that the cutlery is dishwasher safe. Here are some of the best methods we've found for cleaning and polishing flatware and cutlery.

* Always wash pewter and gold-plated flatware by hand and buff dry to bring up the shine and prevent water spots.
* Sterling silver and silver plate may be washed in the dishwasher, but they will need to be polished less often if they are washed by hand. Rinse salt and acid food off flatware as soon as possible to avoid stains.
* Do not soak flatware or cutlery that has bone, ivory, or wood handles; and do not wash them in the dishwasher.
* Use silver often; it tarnishes less and grows more beautiful with use. Store silver and gold flatware in rolls, bags, or cases made with tarnish-resistant cloth.
* Do not allow stainless-steel flatware to touch anything made of silver in the dishwasher. It will set up an electrolytic action that pits the stainless steel and leaves black spots on the silver.
* Wash flatware and cutlery with liquid dishwashing detergent. Fill the sink with hot water, add the detergent, and wash the flatware using a soft cloth or sponge to wipe away the soil. Never use an abrasive cleanser, steel-wool pad, or synthetic scouring pad. Avoid overcrowding the sink to prevent scratching your flatware. After it is clean, rinse with hot water, and buff with a soft towel to bring up the shine.
* Give silverware a quick polish: Sprinkle some baking soda on a damp cloth or a sponge. Rub, rinse, and let dry.
* Shine up your silverware with a banana peel. Remove any leftover "strings" from the inside of the peel, then rub the peel on cutlery and serving pieces. Buff with a clean, soft cloth or a paper towel.
* Make a paste of cornstarch and water and apply to tarnished silverware. Let dry; wipe clean with a dry cloth.
* If you need clean silver now instead of tomorrow morning, pour lemon juice over the piece. Polish with a soft, clean cotton cloth.
* To clean sterling silver pieces and bring back their shine, rub them with a paste made of 1/2 cup distilled white vinegar and 2 tablespoons salt. Dip a clean, soft cloth in the paste, then gently rub silver pieces using a circular motion. Rinse, then dry with another soft cloth.
* Place 1 or 2 pieces of white chalk in your silverware chest to prevent tarnishing.
* Save the outer leaves from a head of cabbage and use them to polish pewter flatware. Rub the leaf over the surface of the pewter, and then buff with a soft cloth.

SILVER POLISH

To remove silver tarnish, bring a medium-size pot of water to a boil and add 1/2 teaspoon salt and 1 to 2 teaspoons baking soda. Reduce heat. Place tarnished silverware and a piece of aluminum foil in the pot. Simmer for 2 to 3 minutes. Rinse the silverware well, then use a soft cloth to buff dry.

GOLD POLISH

Place 1 teaspoon baking soda in a small bowl; add enough water to make a paste. Using a soft cloth, rub the paste over the gold-plated flatware. Rinse and buff dry with a soft cloth or chamois.

STAINLESS STEEL POLISH

Sprinkle baking soda on the wet surface and scrub with a soft cloth or sponge. Wipe with a damp cloth and buff with a soft, dry cloth.

POTS, PANS, & KNIVES

When was the last time you saw your face reflected in the bottom of a skillet or reveled in the warm glow of a copper pot you had just shined? If you can't remember, you probably have much too much to do to worry about keeping your pots, pans, and cooking utensils looking like new. Unless they're on display, a reasonably clean cooking pot functions just about as well as a sparkling clean one does. The amount of shine on your cookware is totally up to you.

Basic care for all cookware starts with reading the manufacturer's care instructions. Wash all pots and pans thoroughly inside and out soon after use. An exception to this is your omelet pan. Clean seasoned omelet pans with a paper towel. If baked-on food necessitates washing the pan in soapsuds, dry it thoroughly over a warm burner and rub vegetable oil into the warm pan with a pad of folded paper toweling.

Prevent heat stains on the outsides of pans by keeping gas flames low so that they cannot lick up the sides. Do not subject cookware to sudden temperature changes. Allow it to cool before washing or soaking.

We recommend that you clean scorched pans by bringing 1 teaspoon baking soda and 1 cup water to boil in the pan. Allow the pan to cool and wash it in soapy water. Substitute vinegar for baking soda to clean scorched aluminum pans.

* Burned-on grease in a pot or pan can be removed by filling the pan with water and adding 6 Alka-Seltzer tablets. Let the pan soak for at least an hour, then scrub it clean.
* To loosen baked- or dried-on food in a pan, gently boil water and baking soda in the pan. When food is loosened, allow pan to cool and then wipe clean.
* Don't struggle to scrape off burned-on food in a pan. Pour in a can of Pepsi; allow pan to soak for about an hour, then wipe clean.
* Get rid of excess grease in a roasting pan by sprinkling it with salt and wiping with a damp sponge or paper towel. Wash as usual.
* Reduce the chore of washing a greasy baking dish or pan. After the grease is drained off, rub the pan with a thick slice of lemon or a used lemon half turned inside out. Wash as usual.

* To remove rust from knives, cast-iron pots, and other kitchen equipment, make a paste with 1 part lemon juice and 2 parts salt. Apply with a clean, soft cloth and rub away the rust. Rinse with clear water; dry well.

* Get rid of rust on a kitchen knife by cutting an onion. Using the rusted blade, carefully cut into (but not all the way through) a large, whole onion. Repeat 2 or 3 times. If there is a large amount of rust on the blade, it may require a few more strokes to clean it off.

* To make stains vanish from aluminum or enamel cookware, fill the pot or pan with water and add a cut lime. Boil until the stains are gone. For a small pot, use half a lime; for a larger one, use both halves.

* The only way to protect aluminum cookware from discoloration is never to wash it in an automatic dishwasher or let it soak in soapy water for long periods of time.
We recommend that you don't allow food to stand in aluminum cookware and don't use it to store food; food that is acid-based can discolor or pit the metal.

* Use a steel-wool soap pad to remove burned-on food from cast-aluminum cookware. Liquid nonabrasive bathroom cleanser or a paste of baking soda and water used with a synthetic scouring pad will polish both cast and sheet aluminum.

* Cast-iron cookware has a tendency to rust if it is not kept properly seasoned. Some new cast-iron cooking utensils come from the factory already sealed, but most will have to be seasoned before their first use.

* Season cast-iron cookware in the traditional way: Scour your pot with a steel-wool soap pad, then wipe the inside with vegetable oil, place it in a warm oven for two hours, and wipe off the excess oil. To maintain your cookware's seasoning, repeat this procedure periodically and whenever rust spots appear.

* After seasoning a cast-iron skillet with a drop of vegetable oil, store it between 2 coffee filters to help keep moisture at bay.

* Wash cast-iron cookware in hot, sudsy water, then dry it thoroughly and store it in a dry cupboard without its lid in place. Never wash cast-iron cookware in the dishwasher; it will remove the seasoning and cause rust.

* Copper darkens with use and exposure to air. If you prefer shiny copper, you can clean and polish it easily. Copper cookware is lined with other metals to prevent harmful chemical reactions with food. The lining is usually tin or stainless steel. If your copper pot has a tin lining, you must be careful not to scrape away the tin by stirring with sharp metal cooking utensils. You can have a copper pan retinned when the lining begins to

wear thin, but this is an expensive procedure. Use wood, nylon, or nonstick-coated spoons for stirring to prevent scratching the lining of copper cookware.

* Some copper cookware comes with a protective lacquer coating that must be removed before the utensil is heated. Follow the manufacturer's instructions, or place the utensil in a solution of 1 cup baking soda and 2 gallons boiling water, let it stand until the water is cool, peel off the lacquer, wash, rinse, and dry.

* Protect copper pans from scorching by making sure there is always liquid or fat in the pan before it is placed on the heat. When melting butter, swirl it around in the bottom of the pan and up the sides. Lower the heat as soon as the contents of the pot reach the boiling point.

* Commercial copper-cleaning products do a good job of cleaning and shining copper cookware if you follow the manufacturer's instructions.

* Nonstick finishes or coatings are relatively thin and damage easily. We recommend that you use wood, nylon, or specially coated spoons and spatulas to prevent surface damage. Most nonstick-coated cookware can be safely washed in the dishwasher.

* Wash new nonstick pans before using them and lightly coat the inside with vegetable oil. Apply vegetable oil again after each washing in the dishwasher and after treating stains, following the procedure described above. Do not soak pans in soapy water; the coating can retain a soap flavor.

MAKE IT YOURSELF! CLEANER FOR DISCOLORED ALUMINUM COOKWARE

To remove interior discoloration, fill the pan with water, add 1 tablespoon cream of tartar or 1 tablespoon lemon juice per quart of water, and simmer until the discoloration is gone. Complete the cleaning process by scouring the pan with a steel-wool soap pad. **Caution:** Wear rubber gloves.

COPPER POLISH

To clean a discolored copper pot, use a paste of 1 tablespoon salt, 1 tablespoon white vinegar, and 1 tablespoon flour. **Caution:** Wear rubber gloves. Because the vinegar is acid, wash the pot in hot soapy water and rinse it. Then buff vigorously for shiny results. (You'll have the same success with a paste made of 2 tablespoons lemon juice and 1 tablespoon salt.)

CLEANER FOR NONSTICK COOKWARE

When you want to remove stains from nonstick-coated cookware, mix 2 table-spoons baking soda with 1 cup water and ½ cup liquid bleach. Boil the solution in the pan for several minutes until the stains disappear. After washing the pan, wipe the inner surface with cooking oil to season it.

YOUR KITCHEN FLOORS

The first step in cleaning any kind of kitchen floor is to reach for your vacuum cleaner. Whether it's a handheld, lightweight cordless, or upright canister, your vacuum cleaner doesn't just push dirt around the floor, it gets rid of it. When you vacuum a floor before you mop it, there's no loose dirt left on the floor to become mud when it's mixed with your floor-cleaning solution, and no loose dirt to scratch the floor as it is being mopped. To accelerate kitchen-floor cleaning, use your vacuum cleaner to clean dirt from the floor, then use your mop to wash the floor.

A vacuum-cleaner crevice tool or a small-brush attachment cleans around baseboards and radiators in the kitchen, just as it does in the rest of the house. But a crevice tool is especially effective in the kitchen, where you can use it to clean places you might not otherwise be able to reach. Use it to remove crumbs from the floor under the range, to get at dust that settles behind the refrigerator, and to clean other dirty, hard-to-reach places.

The following solution is recommended for asphalt, linoleum, rubber-tile, vinyl, and "no-wax" vinyl floors.

MAKE IT YOURSELF!

ONE-STEP FLOOR CLEANER/POLISH

Mix ½ cup vinegar, 2 tablespoons furniture polish, and 1 gallon of warm water. **Caution:** Wear rubber gloves. Mop the floor with this mixture, using a sponge mop or string mop.

Bathroom, restroom, watercloset, loo—whatever you call it, you have to keep it clean. If there's a growing collection of dust balls under your bed or a month's worth of newspapers on your coffee table, you can live with that. But if there is one cleaning job that really must be done each week no matter what, it's cleaning the bathroom.

You can make this unpleasant task a whole lot easier if you and everyone else who uses the bathroom quick-cleans it every day. Most bathrooms are made of materials that are easy to keep clean. Tile and porcelain surfaces are stain-resistant if dirt and scum are not allowed to build up on them. Make it a firm rule in your home to rinse out the tub or shower stall immediately after you use it. Rinse it while you are still wet and in the tub or stall. Simply spray water from the shower head on all interior surfaces, then lather soap onto a damp sponge, swish it around the tub or stall, and rinse. The basin can be given a similar treatment each evening by the last person who uses it.

Keeping tile and porcelain surfaces clean so that they never need to be scoured not only saves time, but it also protects these surfaces from unnecessary wear and keeps them looking their best.

The obvious solution to bathroom clutter is to create storage for the things most bathrooms are not designed to store, such as hair dryers, makeup, electric shavers, and magazines. Clear countertops not only look cleaner, but they are quicker to clean, because there's no clutter to clean around and under.

MILD SURFACE CLEANERS

* Try this basic cleanser for everyday bathroom cleanup. Mix together 3 tablespoons baking soda, 1/2 cup ammonia, and 2 cups warm water. Or skip the ammonia and mix 1 box (16 ounces) baking soda, 4 tablespoons Dawn dishwashing liquid, and 1 cup warm water. Mix well and store in a clearly labeled spray or squeeze container. Be sure to wear rubber gloves and use in a well-ventilated area.

* To keep the bathtub and tiles free of soap scum, rinse thoroughly after each use, and rub the surfaces with a cut lemon. The same method—rubbing surfaces with a cut lemon—can remove many sink and tub rust stains.

* Undiluted bleach in a spray bottle tackles serious bathroom grime. Spray the tub, sink, ceramic tile, or shower surfaces, wait a few minutes, and wipe clean with a damp sponge.

MAKE IT YOURSELF!

BATHROOM CLEANER

This solution cleans porcelain as well as cultured-marble and fiberglass fixtures. Mix 1/2 cup vinegar, 1 cup clear ammonia, and 1/4 cup baking soda in 1 gallon hot water. **Caution:** Wear rubber gloves, and work in a well-ventilated area when using this powerful solution. Apply the solution to the fixtures with a sponge, scrubbing if necessary, and rinse with clear water.

COUNTERTOPS

Bathroom countertops are sloshed, splotched, and splattered with everything from hair spray to shoe polish. In most homes, countertops are made of materials that can stand up to the assault: ceramic tile, cultured marble, and plastic laminate. Because these materials are durable, they are easy to clean.

MAKE IT YOURSELF!

CERAMIC TILE CLEANER

To clean ceramic tile, mix ½ cup vinegar, 1 cup clear ammonia, 1/4 cup baking soda, and 1 gallon warm water. **Caution:** Wear rubber gloves, and work in a well-ventilated area when using this powerful solution. Apply it to the counter-top with a sponge, and rinse with clear water. Wipe dry to prevent water spots. Mix a fresh batch of this cleaner for each cleaning session.

Cultured marble resembles real marble, but it is a lot more versatile and much easier to care for. Unlike plastic laminate, cultured marble is not a thin veneer; if you scratch or burn it, you can often repair the damage.

We recommend that you avoid using abrasive cleaners and steel-wool pads to clean cultured marble; they will scratch the surface, making it difficult to keep clean. Mildly abrasive liquid and powdered cleansers should be applied directly to the wet surface of the countertop to dissolve dirt and soap film. Rinse well, and buff dry with a soft cloth.

Dirt and soap film are quickly and inexpensively removed from cultured marble with this mixture. Mix ½ cup vinegar, 1 cup ammonia, and 1/4 cup baking soda in 1 gallon hot water. **Caution:** Wear rubber gloves, and work in a well-ventilated area when using this powerful solution. Apply it to the cultured marble with a sponge, rinse with clear water, and buff dry.

Plastic laminate is very durable if you don't scratch it, chip it, knock off its edges, burn it, scrub it, let water seep under it, stain it, or otherwise mistreat it. Plastic laminate is made of thin layers of plastic superimposed on craft paper and overlaid on particle board or plywood. The color of most plastic laminate is only in the top layer. The glossy, matte, or textured surface is also laid on. This is the reason plastic laminate cannot be restored if it is damaged; all its beauty is on the surface.

Regularly apply an appliance wax or light furniture wax to protect and brighten plastic-laminate surfaces.

During your bathroom-cleaning session, wipe your plastic-laminate countertop with a damp cloth or sponge. A two-sided scrubbing pad with fiber on one side and a sponge on the other works especially well. Moistened slightly with water, the fiber side is just abrasive enough to loosen greasy smears and other soil. Turning the scrubber over, use the sponge side to wipe the surface damp-dry.

When a spot or stain persists, first sprinkle baking soda on the spot and scrub gently. If this doesn't take care of the problem, apply a polishing cleanser with a wet sponge.

MILDEW BUSTERS

* When mildew is multiplying in out-of-the-way spots, place a few cotton balls soaked in bleach in the area. Wait a few hours, then wipe clean with a sponge dampened with warm water.

* Mix equal amounts of vinegar and water in a spray bottle. Spray onto mildewed areas and let sit for 15 minutes. Wipe clean.

* Undiluted isopropyl rubbing alcohol can remove small areas of mildew buildup on grout, caulk, or tile. Dip a cloth into the alcohol and scrub.

* Mildew may make a habit of building up on your shower and tub accessories. Mix 1 1/2 cups bleach with 2 gallons water and scrub bath mats, curtains, and soap dishes with the mixture, using a sponge or a scrub brush. Rinse.

SHOWERS & BATHTUBS

* To clean gunky shower tracks, wrap very fine steel wool around an old toothbrush and scrub the tracks. Spray glass cleaner all over the tracks; wipe clean.

* Loosen up soap scum on shower doors and walls by spraying them with vinegar. Let dry, then respray to dampen. Wipe clean. Reapply and let sit for several hours. Then dampen and wipe clean again.

* Shower curtains can become dulled by soap film or plagued with mildew. Keep vinegar in a spray bottle near your shower, and squirt shower curtains once or twice a week. No need to rinse.

* Fight mildew stains and lightly clean a shower curtain by sprinkling baking soda on a sponge and scrubbing. Rinse well.

* To remove mineral and mildew stains from a shower curtain, first soak it in salt water for 15 to 20 minutes. Hang to drain excess water. Rub the stains with lemon juice while the curtain is still damp. Wipe with a damp sponge, rinse with clean water, or run through the washing machine.

* Prevent mildew growth on a shower curtain by soaking it in a bathtub full of salt water (1/2 cup salt to the tub). Soak for several hours, then hang to dry.

* Those sunflower decals may have looked cute when you stuck them on the tub to prevent slips and falls, but now they're chipped, stained, and probably out of fashion. To get rid of them, loosen the glue by saturating each decal with vinegar. (Warm vinegar in microwave for about 3 minutes for better results.) Let vinegar sit for a few minutes, then peel off decals. You should be able to remove any leftover glue by scrubbing with a damp sponge.

MAKE IT YOURSELF!

SHOWER STALL CLEANER

Mix 1/2 cup vinegar, 1 cup ammonia, 1/4 cup baking soda, and 1 gallon hot water. **Caution:** Wear rubber gloves, and work in a well-ventilated area when using this powerful solution. Apply it to the walls of the shower with a sponge, scrubbing with a brush if necessary to remove all the scum. Rinse well with clear water and wipe dry.

SINKS

* Attack stubborn rust stains in a sink (or tub) with a paste of cream of tartar and hydrogen peroxide. Apply the paste, then scrub clean with a nonabrasive pad or brush. Rinse completely.

* A dryer sheet can control odor and musty smells under your bathroom sink.

* Plug the drain in your bathroom sink, pour in 1/2 cup vinegar, then fill the sink with water. Let sit 1 hour, then scrub any mineral deposit areas with an old toothbrush. Rinse.

* Pour isopropyl rubbing alcohol on a paper towel to remove smudges and hairspray from chrome faucets.

* Clean chrome with club soda. Pour some on a clean, soft cloth and dab it on. Buff to a shine with a second cloth.

SINKS

* Attack stubborn rust stains in a sink (or tub) with a paste of cream of tartar and hydrogen peroxide. Apply the paste, then scrub clean with a nonabrasive pad or brush. Rinse completely.

* A dryer sheet can control odor and musty smells under your bathroom sink.

* Plug the drain in your bathroom sink, pour in 1/2 cup vinegar, then fill the sink with water. Let sit 1 hour, then scrub any mineral deposit areas with an old toothbrush. Rinse.

* Pour isopropyl rubbing alcohol on a paper towel to remove smudges and hairspray from chrome faucets.

* Clean chrome with club soda. Pour some on a clean, soft cloth and dab it on. Buff to a shine with a second cloth.

GROUT

* For tough grout or tile stains, use a paste of 1 part bleach to 3 parts baking soda.

* Use a paste of baking soda and water to remove mildew stains on grout. Apply, scrub with an old toothbrush, and rinse.

* For everyday cleaning of tile and grout, rub with a little apple cider vinegar on a sponge. This gives off a pleasant scent and will help cut any greasy buildup.

Grout grime grating on you? Combine the following in a bucket: 2 cups bleach, 3 cups isopropyl rubbing alcohol, 1/2 cup Original Pine-Sol Brand Cleaner, and 1 quart water. Pour the mixture into a plastic spray bottle. Spray and clean away!

DEODORIZING

* Sprinkle baking soda in the bathroom trash can after each emptying.

* Add a perpetual air freshener to the toilet area by keeping baking soda in a pretty dish on top of the tank. Add your favorite scented bath salts to the mix if desired. Change every 3 months.

* When you hang a new roll of toilet paper, loosely roll up a dryer sheet and place it inside the paper core. The fresh scent will disperse through the small room.

Indoor plumbing was becoming a "fixture" by about 1870, replacing chamber pots, buckets, and portable washing basins. As early as 1778, Joseph Bramah of London invented the metal valve-type water closet. Other early sinks, toilets, and bathtubs also were made of metal—primarily lead, copper, and zinc. They were hard to clean, however, so in the mid-1870s Thomas Twyford made a ceramic toilet and wash-down water closet. Because ceramics are too brittle for bathtubs, the porcelain-enamel cast-iron tub was invented. The double-shell, built-in style still common today was introduced around 1915.

TOILETS

Cleaning the toilet is one of those grin-and-bear-it chores that you want to get through as quickly as possible. Many toilet-bowl cleaners and deodorizers claim that they'll help you do this. Some products are truly helpful, some are not. Most cleaners that are placed in the tank and are dispensed each time the toilet is flushed do little more than color the water. Some clean the bowl better than plain water, but in-tank cleaners are not a substitute for a regular scrubbing, when you also clean the seat and the rim of the toilet bowl.

Toilet bowls and tanks usually are made of vitreous china, which is nonporous and easy to clean. Before you clean your toilet, read the label on your cleaning product to learn its exact chemical makeup and how it should be used. Be especially careful never to mix products that contain chlorine bleach with ammonia-based products. Always wear rubber gloves when you work with toilet cleaners. They contain strong chemicals and should be flushed immediately after the bowl has been cleaned. You should be careful not to allow cleaners to remain in the toilet or to touch other bathroom surfaces.

We suggest that you keep a long-handled brush for cleaning only toilet bowls. The exterior of a toilet should be cleaned with the same products you use for tubs and basins. Wipe the toilet seat, the tank, around the rim, and around the base when you clean.

* Once a week, pour 2 cups vinegar into toilet and let it sit. (Tip: Rest toilet bowl brush inside bowl with lid closed to remind yourself and family members not to use the toilet until it gets brushed!) After 8 hours or more, brush toilet well; flush. This regular treatment will keep hard-water stains at bay and clean and freshen your bowl between major cleanings.
* A half cup of baking soda in the toilet bowl will work for light cleaning. Let sit for 30 minutes, then brush and flush.
* Remove stubborn stains in the toilet bowl by scrubbing with fine steel wool dipped in baking soda.
* To remove toilet bowl stains, pour in a can of Pepsi. Wait 1 hour, then brush bowl clean and flush.
* Clean your toilet by putting 2 denture cleanser tablets in the bowl and letting them sit overnight. Scrub the toilet in the morning.

✳ Clean your toilet while you're not even home! Pour 1/4 cup bleach into the bowl, but don't flush the toilet until you return—even days later. (Be sure to close the bathroom door before you leave if pets will be around.)

DRAINS

In most homes, the bathroom sink is a dressing table as well as a washbasin, and everyone in the family shampoos in the shower. Hair and soap are washed into bathroom drains day and night, and the cruddy mess can quickly jam up the works. All that is needed to clean some clogged drains is to clear the trap of hair and soap curds. Regular clearing of the traps saves your plumbing, and it also cuts down on cleaning time, since when water flows out of the basin and tub quickly, it doesn't allow dirt to settle on these surfaces.

When clearing the trap doesn't clear the drain, you'll have to take stronger measures. First, use a plumber's helper and plunge the drain. (We suggest that you keep one handy in the bathroom.) Before you use the plunger in the bathroom basin, plug the overflow opening. This allows the plunger to exercise its maximum suction effect on the sadly clogged drain.

Ancient Cleaning Secrets

Around 600 B.C., the Phoenicians made soap from goat's tallow (fat) and wood ashes; they sometimes used it as an article of barter with the Gauls.

The Celts used animal fats and plant ashes and named the product *saipo,* from which the English word soap is derived.

Beginning in the second century A.D., at the suggestion of the Greek physician Galen, soap was used for washing and cleaning (instead of as a medicine).

Clear a slow drain by dropping in a couple of Alka-Seltzer tablets. Pour in 1 cup vinegar, then flush with hot water.

To clear a slow drain, pour in a 2-liter bottle of Pepsi. You'll soon see the drain emptying more quickly.

For routine cleaning of sink and tub drains, pour in 1/2 cup baking soda followed by 1 cup distilled white vinegar. Let sit for 10 to 20 minutes, then flush with very hot water.

Moderately clogged drains sometimes can be opened by pouring 1/2 cup baking soda, followed by 1/2 cup vinegar down the drain. **Caution:** The interaction of these two ingredients creates foaming and fumes, so replace the drain cover loosely. Flush the drain with clear water after about 3 hours.

If plunging does not open the drain, use a chemical drain opener. These products must be handled with special care because they are caustic and harmful to skin and eyes. Use them in a well-ventilated area, and follow the manufacturer's instructions. Commercial drain openers are sold in granular, liquid, and pressurized forms. Granular products utilize lye to do their work, liquid drain openers use lye and other chemicals, and pressurized products work by chlorofluoro-carbon propellants and pressure. If you use a granular drain opener, you must first remove standing water from the sink; this is not necessary for liquid and pressurized products.

Chemical drain openers will damage porcelain enamel and should not be allowed to remain on the surface of your fixtures for any length of time.

If the first type of chemical drain opener you use does not work, do not use a different chemical drain cleaner unless the initial cleaner has been flushed away totally. Never use a plunger or a pressurized drain opener after using a chemical cleaner; it may cause dangerous chemicals to splash back onto you. Also, be sure to tell your plumber what you have put into the drain before he or she starts to work. The combination of ammonia and other household cleaners with chemical drain openers produces hazardous gases.

MAKE IT YOURSELF!

MIRROR CLEANERS

Mix 1 1/3 cup clear ammonia in 1 gallon warm water. Apply it with a sponge/squeegee, or pour the solution into a spray container and spray it directly onto the mirror. Buff with a lint-free cloth, chamois, or paper toweling. Vinegar may be substituted for ammonia.

Pour vinegar into a shallow bowl or pan, then crumple a sheet of newspaper, dip it in the vinegar, and apply to the mirror. Wipe the glass several times with the same newspaper until the mirror is almost dry, then shine it with a clean, soft cloth or dry newspaper.

Mix 2 cups isopropyl rubbing alcohol (70-percent solution), 2 tablespoons liquid dishwashing detergent, and 2 cups water. Stir until thoroughly mixed and then pour into a spray bottle. Spray directly onto the mirror. Buff with a lint-free cloth, chamois, or paper toweling.

A FEW LAST TIPS

* Wish you could turn those slippery slivers of soap into something other than trash? Collect them in a sandwich-size food storage bag. When the bag is about half full, place it in a pot of warm—but not boiling—water. Remove when the soap melts. When it cools, you'll have a new bar of soap.

* Alternately, whenever a bar becomes too small to handle, cut slits in a sponge and tuck in the soap pieces. Or, put the slivers in a clean child-size sock to make a soaped-up washcloth. Both are perfect for your child's bath time.

* Bring some order to that bathroom or bedroom drawer. A plastic ice cube tray is the perfect organizer for small items such as bobby pins, hair clips, safety pins, earrings, rings, and spare change.

* A large binder clip placed on the end of a tube of toothpaste or similar packaging will ensure that you'll get all your money's worth.

* Soak toothbrushes overnight in a solution of 4 tablespoons baking soda to 1 quart warm water.

* Soak dentures, athletic mouthguards, retainers, or other oral appliances in a solution of 2 teaspoons baking soda dissolved in a glass of warm water. Another option is to scrub these items using an old toothbrush dipped in baking soda.

* So that you won't misplace frequently used items, glue small magnets on the walls of the medicine cabinet to hold nail files, cuticle scissors, clippers, and other small metal objects.

* Your medicine cabinet will stay neat and clean with shelf paper made of blotters that can absorb medicine or cosmetic spills.

Your bundle of joy can unfortunately produce bundles of mess. And when you're the parent of a baby or toddler, you have a lot of demands on your time and energy. These hacks can help.

GENERAL TIPS

✳ Sprinkle baking soda on a damp sponge to wipe down cribs, changing tables, baby mattresses, and playpens. Rinse areas thoroughly and allow to dry.

✳ Remove odors from cloth strollers or car seats by sprinkling baking soda on the fabric. Wait 15 minutes (longer for strong odors) and vacuum.

✳ Use baking soda directly on metal, plastic, or vinyl strollers, car seats, and high chairs. Scrub using a damp sponge. Rinse and wipe dry.

✳ Split open the seams of one or two trash bags; place on the floor under a high chair. Why spend money on an expensive store-bought drop cloth?

DIAPER CONTROL

✳ Keep diaper pails smelling fresh by sprinkling baking soda over dirty cloth diapers. Line the bottom of a diaper pail with baking soda after you empty it to control odors.

✳ Accidents happen, especially during potty training. In lieu of a plastic or rubber mattress pad, place several sheets of aluminumf oil across the width of a mattress. Cover them with a beach towel or two, then put on a cloth mattress pad and bottom sheet.

* To remove urine from a mattress, first blot dry with a towel or rag. Then sprinkle area with baking soda. Let dry thoroughly, then vacuum.

TOYS

* Clean and deodorize vinyl toys with a solution of 1 tablespoon baking soda per cup of water. Wash toys with a damp cloth or sponge, rinse, and dry. For tough stain removal, sprinkle baking soda directly on a damp sponge and scrub. Bring a small spray bottle of this same baking soda solution with you on outings with baby for quick cleanups.

* Disinfect baby toys by cleaning them with a splash of vinegar added to hot water or by soaking them in a dishpan of hot water and 1/2 cup distilled white vinegar.

* Cloth toys can get grungy. To clean without water, sprinkle on baking soda as a dry shampoo; let sit 15 minutes, then brush off.

* Deodorize really smelly stuffed animals by placing them in a paper bag, adding baking soda, and shaking the closed bag vigorously. Store in bag overnight. If necessary, change the baking soda and repeat until odor is gone.

* Here's another method for cleaning stuffed animals or other cuddlies: Place a toy or a few small ones into a medium to large plastic bag. Add some cornstarch to the bag, close tightly, and shake. Brush the toys clean.

CLOTHING

* If your baby spits up on his shirt or yours, moisten a cloth, dip it in baking soda, and dab at the spot. The odor will be controlled until the clothing can be changed.

* For tough stains on baby clothes, soak the items (colorfast only) in a bucket of water with 1/4 cup bleach added. Wait 10 minutes, rinse in clean water, then launder as usual.

MAKE THINGS SMELL GOOD

Despite your best efforts to keep things clean, sometimes you still walk down into the basement, open a closet, or return from vacation and think that you smell something musty in your house. Here are some tips to help.

THROUGHOUT THE HOUSE

* Combine 1 teaspoon baking soda, 1 tablespoon vinegar, and 2 cups water. Stir; mixture will foam up a bit but this will soon subside. Store the solution in a clearly labeled spray bottle. Spray a mist in the air anywhere you want to eliminate or control household odors.

* Pour vinegar into shallow bowls and set them out to absorb odors in areas of your home where odors are a problem. Make sure the bowls are out of reach of small children and pets.

* To make a homemade air freshener, fill a coffee filter with baking soda and close it with a twist tie. Place it where the air is less than fresh—in the refrigerator, closet, your car, shoes, boots, or anywhere.

Baking soda is a naturally occurring, very versatile substance that's environmentally safe and inexpensive. Not only is baking soda nontoxic, it's actually a food, so—unlike many commercial household products—it is safe to use around children and pets.

GARBAGE CANS

✳ Periodically wash out and deodorize garbage cans with a solution of 1 cup baking soda per gallon of water.

✳ Reduce garbage can smells by sprinkling baking soda inside each time you add garbage.

✳ Before you replace the trash bag in a stinky garbage can or diaper pail, pour some non clumping cat litter in the bottom. When the litter gets damp, change it.

✳ When you put out your trash in plastic bags, coat the outside of the bags with a little ammonia. The smell should keep strays away. Consider spraying the outside of your trash cans with ammonia too.

PAPER

✳ To clean musty items such as old postcards, magazines, sheet music, and books, place the items in a paper bag with some baking powder. Seal bag and change powder every few days until odor disappears.

✳ You can refresh musty old magazines found in cellars or garages if the pages aren't stuck together. Just lay the magazines out in the sun for a day. Then sprinkle baking soda on the pages and let sit for an hour or so. Brush off.

✳ Dry out the moisture in a damp book by sprinkling the pages with cornstarch and letting it sit overnight. Brush out the cornstarch in the morning. This even works on mildewed books. Cover the mildew spots with cornstarch and let sit for a few days. Brush off the powder outdoors, so the mildew spores won't find a new home in your home.

✳ Cat litter will freshen up musty-smelling items, such as books or old magazines. Put the items in a paper bag; carefully pour in about 1 cup litter. Check on the progress and replace the litter every other day till the job's done.

✳ Reduce the dampness and prevent mildew in a closet or basement with white chalk. Tie together 12 sticks with a string or put several sticks in a knee high pantyhose. Hang the chalk in the damp area; replace every few months.

✳ A closet with bare wood floors can begin to smell stale. To freshen the whole closet, lightly mop the floor with a mixture of 1 cup baking soda and 1/2 cup vinegar in 1 gallon warm water.

✳ Deodorize a closet by placing a shallow box of cat litter on the floor—even if you don't have a cat. Keep the door shut. In a few days, the air should be fresher.

✳ Turn your closet into a cedar closet. Fill a large plastic food storage almost to the top with cedar chips (available at pet stores). Seal the bag and poke small holes all over both sides. Hang it in your closet.

✳ Make a sachet for dresser drawers: Pour potpourri into the toe portion of pantyhose or knee highs. Tie a knot right above the potpourri and cut off the remainder of the hosiery.

✳ The enticing aroma of herbal tea suits a sachet perfectly. Choose your favorite flavor or scent, open a tea bag or two, and pour the leaves into pantyhose or knee highs. Tie a knot right above the tea and cut off the remainder of the hosiery.

✳ Fill the toes of an old pair of pantyhose with baking soda, cut off the legs, and tie to secure. Hang the sachets anywhere musty odors linger.

✳ To keep dressers, sideboards, and linen closets smelling nice, grab a few new, unwrapped bars of bar soap. Wrap each in facial tissue and place them in drawers and on shelves.

✳ Fill a snack- or sandwich-size food storage bag with potpourri. Seal it and poke several small holes to make an effective yet inexpensive sachet for your dresser drawers.

✳ Eliminate mildew odors in drawers and on various other surfaces by wiping the affected area with full-strength antiseptic mouthwash. Wipe clean with a paper towel.

✳ If your cedar chest or closet no longer smells of cedar, lightly sand its surfaces. Sanding opens the wood's pores and releases a fresh cedar scent. Remember that the scent doesn't kill moths; it merely repels them. So it's best to clean clothes before storing to remove any moth eggs.

BAGS, TRUNKS, HAMPERS, & MORE

✳ To combat the aroma inside an odor-collector such as a laundry hamper, shoe, or diaper pail, place a dryer sheet inside it.

✳ Deodorize a canvas bag or any bag that has developed a musty smell by sprinkling the inside with salt, zipping up the bag, and letting it sit overnight. Shake out the salt in the morning and allow bag to air out.

✳ An old trunk can smell mighty musty. To get rid of the odor, haul the trunk outside for some sunlight and fresh air. Pour a light layer of baking powder in the bottom and close the lid. Every few days, sweep out the old and sprinkle on some new powder. Repeat until the smell is gone.

✳ If that old trunk smells stale and musty when you open it, empty it out and give it a little fresh air. Let it sit outside in the sunshine, open wide, for several hours. When you bring the trunk inside, sprinkle a layer of cat litter on the bottom and close the lid. Replace the litter every other day until the odor is gone.

✳ Control odors in shoes that are starting to smell by sprinkling the insides with a little salt. Let sit overnight, then shake out the salt. The salt will help control moisture, which contributes to odors.

✳ Tuck dryer sheets under your chair or couch cushions to help freshen furniture.

✳ You can also pack a dryer sheet in your suitcase or gym bag. It will protect your clean clothes from the odors of your dirty ones.

✳ Control odor from a pet accident by leaving a thin layer of baking soda on the affected area after cleaning. Vacuum when dry.

WHILE ON VACATION

✳ If your bathroom never seems to be fully dry and you are going away for some time, place a large, shallow box of nonclumping cat litter in your bathtub to absorb moisture.

✳ If you're going away for the weekend, deodorize your fridge while you're gone. Just pour some clean cat litter onto a cookie sheet and place it on the middle shelf of the fridge. Discard upon your return.

✳ If you own a summer cabin or other building that will be shut up for a long period of time, prevent damp, musty odors from taking over while you're gone by filling shallow boxes with cat litter and storing one in each room of the house.

Most of us ignore our ceilings until cobwebs hang down so far they block our view of the television or until we're flat on our backs with flu. When we finally look up, we're likely to see a grayish, brownish haze, combining the smoke of burned toast with cooking grease and all kinds of airborne particles. If your ceiling has lost its original color, you'll have to brush away the cobwebs and wipe away the smog. It's not something you need to do very often, but we're here to help you when the time comes.

A few basic tips for ceiling cleaning:

*   Lift cobwebs off ceilings with your vacuum cleaner and its brush attachment. Be careful not to crush cobwebs onto the ceiling; they will leave black smudge marks.
*   Wash or clean ceilings before walls if you are cleaning the whole room. But watch out for drips; if you allow drips to run down walls, they may leave permanent marks.
*   Protect furniture and floors with plastic drop cloths or newspaper while you clean the ceiling.
*   Use a sponge mop to clean ceilings so you won't need a ladder.

ACOUSTICAL TILE & SUSPENDED PANEL

Acoustical ceiling treatments are made of porous materials to absorb noise. You can wash vinyl-coated acoustical ceilings. Use an all-purpose cleaning solution applied with a sponge mop. Noncoated tiles generally are not washable, but you can spot-clean them, using special products available at hardware stores. When an overall cleaning is needed, we recommend an application of acoustical-tile paint.

PAINTED

The most frequently used ceiling paint is latex, which is easy to wash after it has "cured," or set for a period of time. The other kind of paint used on ceiling is alkyd, or oil-based; it is durable and washable and comes in three finishes: flat, semigloss, and gloss. Flat and semigloss are most often used on ceilings, but some bathroom and kitchen ceilings are gloss.

We recommend that you clean painted ceilings with commercial liquid or powdered all-purpose cleaners, following the manufacturer's instructions, rinse with clear water, and allow to dry.

MAKE IT YOURSELF!

PAINTED-CEILING CLEANER

Mix ½ cup vinegar, 1 cup clear ammonia, ¼ cup baking soda, and 1 gallon warm water. **Caution:** Wear rubber gloves, and work in a well-ventilated area when using this solution. Apply it to the ceiling with a sponge and rinse with clear water.

PAPERED

Paper-covered ceilings are not washable. When you need to clean them, we recommend that you use a commercial wallpaper cleaning product and follow the manufacturer's instructions for the best results.

We've found that you can remove smudges from papered ceilings by very gently rubbing the spots with an art gum eraser. General soil comes off when a piece of rye bread is wadded up and used like an eraser. To clean a grease spot, blot it with paper toweling and gently press cornstarch on the stain. After the cornstarch absorbs the grease, rub it off gently.

Many ceilings are "papered" with washable vinyl. Some manufacturers of vinyl wall-coverings caution against using ammonia-based cleaners. Be sure to check the instructions for cleaning your particular ceiling, or test your ceiling covering in an inconspicuous area before you attempt to clean the entire surface.

MAKE IT YOURSELF!

VINYL-COVERED CEILING CLEANERS

Mix ½ cup vinegar and 1 quart water. Gently apply the solution to the ceiling with a sponge. **Caution:** Wear rubber gloves when you work with this cleaner. Don't let the ceiling get too wet; moisture could seep under the seams and loosen the backing of the vinyl.

You can make a "dry detergent" to clean vinyl ceiling coverings. Mix ¼ cup dish-washing liquid with 1 cup warm water in a mixing bowl and beat the solution with an eggbeater to a stiff foam. Working in a small area, dip a sponge into the foam and apply it to the ceiling to loosen dirt. Rinse the detergent with a sponge dipped in clear water and squeezed dry.

PLASTER

Decorative plaster ceilings, as opposed to flat, painted plaster ceilings, can't be cleaned because of their unpainted surface and deep texture. When a plaster ceiling becomes dirty, the best treatment is first to vacuum it, using a brush attachment on your vacuum cleaner, and then to respray it with plaster.

SPRAY-ON ACOUSTICAL FINISH

This rough, sound-absorbing finish is often used in new construction and remodeling. Spray-on acoustical finishes are relatively inexpensive and quick to apply. They cover cracks and other ceiling imperfections. But this kind of ceiling can't be cleaned. When the ceiling becomes dirty, the best thing to do is to vacuum it, using a brush attachment on your vacuum cleaner. Then respray it with a thin coat of the original finish. You can rent spray equipment at most paint stores.

TILE

Vinyl-coated ceiling tile can be cleaned with an all-purpose cleaning solution. Nonwashable tiles can be spot-cleaned with products available at most hardware and paint stores. When an overall cleaning is needed, paint the tiles with either latex or oil-based paint.

CLEANING WALLS

Walls get dirty in the same passive way that ceilings do: Grime and dust float through the air, land on them, and stick. But walls also get dirty in more active ways—when toddlers try out their crayons, chocolate-bar eaters switch on lights, and exuberant chefs toss spaghetti. Unless you deal with the passive dirt buildup on walls, attempts to wipe up after your active family will result in a smeary mess or leave a streak of clean-wall color in sharp contrast to the rest of your wall.

The first known use of the military phrase "spit and polish," indicating the extra effort exerted to get an article clean, was recorded in 1895.

* Use your vacuum cleaner with a floor/wall brush to vacuum your walls whenever you clean the room. Go behind pictures and mirrors with the small-brush attachment.
* Remove cobwebs carefully. Don't press them against the wall; they'll leave a smudge.
* Use an all-purpose cleaner for cleaning washable walls. We recommend that you test the product by first washing an inconspicuous place to make sure it does not harm your wall. Wash walls from the bottom to the top, overlapping the cleaned areas to prevent streaks.
* We've found that you can keep water from running down your arm when you wash walls by making a bracelet from a sponge or washcloth held in place with a thick rubber band.
* To remove transparent tape from a wall without marring the paint or wallpaper, use a warm iron. Through a protective cloth, press the tape with the iron to soften and loosen its adhesive backing.
* If your young artist has chosen crayon as a medium and a painted wall as a canvas, use a baby wipe to gently erase the marks.

* Remove crayon marks from walls with a damp sponge dipped in baking soda.
* Erase crayon marks and drawings from painted walls by rubbing them with Crest toothpaste on a soft cloth. Rinse away with warm water.
* Cornstarch can remove crayon marks from wallpaper. Mix a little with water to make a thick paste, then dab it on the affected area. Let dry completely, then brush off.

WALLPAPER

Wallpaper is not washable. We recommend that you clean it only with commercial products, following the manufacturer's instructions for the best results. But we've found some simple, quick ways to clean up smears, spots, and writing on the wall between major cleaning.

* Take a grease spot off wallpaper by first blotting it with a paper towel and then applying cornstarch to the area. Gently rub off the corn starch, then vacuum the area using an upholstery brush attachment.
* General soil comes off when a piece of rye bread is wadded up and used like an eraser.
* Baking powder gently but thoroughly removes dirt and grime from delicate wallpaper. Make a paste with water and baking powder and apply it to your wall with a sponge. Wipe clean with another damp sponge.
* Mix 1/2 cup vinegar and 1 quart water and apply solution to dirty wallpaper using a sponge. Be careful not to saturate, especially at seams and corners, or you could loosen wallpaper.

WOOD/WOOD PANELED WALLS

All wood paneling is not finished in the same way, so it is not cleaned in the same way. If your paneling was left natural or stained with a water-based stain and not sealed, the only way you should clean it is with your vacuum cleaner. If your paneling has an oil finish, you can clean it with a commercial oil-based product or our homemade cleaner, but avoid any cleaning product that contains wax. If your paneling has a waxed finish, use only wax-based cleaners.

Using your vacuum cleaner with the wall-brush attachment is the best way to clean loose dirt from all kinds of wood paneling. Never use water to clean wood. If you use a spray or aerosol cleaner/polish, follow the manufacturer's instructions carefully.

＊ Mayonnaise will get rid of white water marks on wood paneling. Rub a small amount into each mark; let soak in overnight, then wipe clean.

＊ Bring out the shine of varnished woodwork with cold Lipton tea. Wipe it onto the wood using a soft cloth; rinse with cool water and a sponge. Dry with a clean cloth.

MAKE IT YOURSELF!

WOOD POLISH

This make-it-yourself polish restores the beauty of wood paneling that has an oil finish. Pour equal parts turpentine and boiled linseed oil into a jar, tighten the lid, and shake the liquid to blend it thoroughly. **Caution:** Wear rubber gloves. Pour a small amount of the mixture onto a soft cloth and rub up and down the paneling, following the grain of the wood. The wood will appear oily, but within an hour the polish will be completely absorbed, leaving a soft sheen on your paneling.

PAINTED WALLS

Most walls are painted with latex, which is easy to wash after it has "cured," or set for a period of time. The other kind of wall paint, alkyd, or oil-based, is more durable than latex, but it is more difficult to apply. Both types of paint come in three finishes: flat, semigloss, and gloss.

Clean painted walls with a commercial all-purpose cleaner or use the following recipe for a homemade cleaner.

If your walls have a rough texture, use old nylon stockings or socks rather than a sponge because they won't tear and leave difficult-to-remove bits on the surface.

✳ Take a grease spot off wallpaper by first blotting it with a paper towel and then applying cornstarch to the area. Gently rub off the cornstarch, then vacuum the area using an upholstery brush attachment.

MAKE IT YOURSELF!

PAINTED-WALL CLEANER

Mix ½ cup vinegar, 1 cup clear ammonia, ¼ cup baking soda, and 1 gallon warm water. **Caution:** Wear rubber gloves, and work in a well-ventilated area when using this powerful solution. Apply the solution to the wall with a sponge and rinse with clear water.

BRICK WALLS

A wall made of brick requires little attention if you use your vacuum cleaner to remove loose dirt regularly. A solution of hot water and an all-purpose cleaner will clean accumulated dirt and stains from the surface.

✳ If the brick wall is especially dirty, use a commercial brick cleaner and a stiff-bristled brush. Rinse with clear, hot water, and wipe dry.

✱ Slight smoke stains above a fireplace opening are quickly removed with abrasive cleanser. Scrub the powder into the moistened brick and then rinse with clear water, making sure no white residue remains. If spot-cleaning changes the color of the brick, you can even out the color by rubbing another brick of the same color over the discolored surface.

CERAMIC TILE

We recommend that you clean both glazed and unglazed ceramic tile regularly with an all-purpose cleaning solution or a spray tile-and-grout cleaner. **Caution:** Use rubber gloves to avoid skin contact, and don't breathe the mist when spraying the tile. Scrub dirt from the grout with a toothbrush or nailbrush, taking care not to scratch the tile. After cleaning, a clear-water rinse is recommended. Then buff with a soft, dry cloth to bring out the shine on glazed tile.

You can clean darkened grout with a solution of ¼ cup liquid chlorine bleach and 1 quart water. Scrub this cleaner into the grout with a toothbrush and rinse with clear water.

Grout can also be cleaned with a paste made from 3 parts baking soda and 1 part water. Apply this to the grout with a damp cloth, scrub with a toothbrush, and rinse with clear water.

MAKE IT YOURSELF!

CERAMIC-TILE CLEANER

Mix ½ cup vinegar, 1 cup clear ammonia, ¼ cup baking soda, and 1 gallon warm water. **Caution:** Wear rubber gloves to protect your hands, and work in a well-ventilated area. Applied to the wall with a sponge, this solution does a wonderful job of cutting grease and cleaning soil. Rinse with clear water.

MIRROR TILE

You clean all mirror tiles in the same way, whether they are clear, smoked, or have a design painted or etched on them.

Use one of the following homemade cleaners; they are as effective as commercial products and cost a lot less. Never use soap on mirror tile; it will streak and leave a film.

MAKE IT YOURSELF!

CLEANERS FOR MIRROR TILE

Mix 1/3 cup clear ammonia in 1 gallon warm water. Apply with a sponge/squeegee or pour the solution into a spray container and spray it directly onto the mirror tiles. **Caution:** Wear rubber gloves. Buff with a lint-free cloth, chamois, or paper toweling. Vinegar may be substituted for ammonia.

Mix 2 cups isopropyl rubbing alcohol (70 percent), 2 tablespoons liquid dish washing detergent, and 2 cups water. Stir the solution until thoroughly mixed, then pour it into a pump bottle, and spray it directly onto the mirror tiles. Buff with a lint-free cloth, chamois, or paper toweling.

Pour vinegar into a shallow bowl or pan, crumple a sheet of newspaper, dip it in the vinegar, and apply to the tile. Wipe the mirror tile several times with the same newspaper until it is almost dry, then shine the tile with a clean, soft cloth or dry newspaper.

DECORATOR TILE

Self-sticking decorator tiles, which are often vinyl-coated, are grease- and stain-resistant. A quick wipe with a sponge dipped in an all-purpose cleaning solution is usually all that is needed to keep them fresh and bright. You should try to avoid excessive moisture; it might seep between the seams and loosen the backing.

METAL TILE

Wipe metal tile with a cloth dampened with an all-purpose cleaner and then buff with a soft, dry cloth to avoid streaking.

VINYL

If your wall coverings are made of vinyl, rather than paper, they're washable. Some manufacturers caution against using ammonia-based cleaners, so be sure to check the instructions for cleaning your vinyl wall covering or test the cleaning product you plan to use on your wall in an inconspicuous area.

You can also use a "dry detergent" to clean a vinyl wall covering. Mix ¼ cup dishwashing liquid with 1 cup warm water in a mixing bowl and beat the mixture to a stiff foam with an eggbeater. Working in a small area, dip a sponge into the foam and apply it to the wall to loosen dirt. Rinse the detergent with a sponge that has been dipped in clear water and squeezed dry.

CLEANER FOR VINYL WALL COVERINGS

Mix ½ cup vinegar and 1 quart water and gently apply the solution to the wall with a sponge. **Caution:** Wear rubber gloves. Don't use too much moisture; it could seep under the seams and loosen the backing.

You can avoid washing your windows by keeping the drapes drawn, the shades down, or the blinds closed. But life without windows is a little gloomy, so we suggest that you plan to wash your windows twice a year, usually in the spring and in the fall. If you get everyone in the household involved in window washing, you can probably finish the task on a Saturday morning. Put some of your crew to work inside and others outside. Tell those who are at work in the house to use vertical strokes; those working on the outside should use horizontal strokes. With this method, you can quickly track down streaks.

Wash windows from the top down to prevent drips on sections you've already cleaned. Use a soft toothbrush or cotton swab to clean corners.

Soap will leave smudges on windowpanes, and abrasive cleansers or steel wool will scratch the glass. Window cleaners themselves pose a threat to woodwork. If the cleaner is allowed to drip on the windowsill, it can harm the paint or varnish.

If you wash windows on a hot or sunny day, the glass is more likely to streak.

WINDOWS

* Wash windows with a sponge dipped in baking soda. To avoid dry haze on the windows, rinse them with a clean sponge and plenty of water before drying.

* Clean your windows with club soda. Pour some on a clean cotton cloth; wipe windows. Using a second cloth, dry them right away.

* To spot-clean a window or other glass surface, use isopropyl rubbing alcohol.

* Wash greasy kitchen windows with a solution of 2 tablespoons lemon juice, 1/2 cup distilled white vinegar, and 1 quart warm water.

* The simplest and easiest method of making window cleaner is to add 2 tablespoons vinegar to 1 cup water. Spray solution on windows, and wipe with paper towels.

* Washing a window with intricate panes? Dip a Q-tips cottonswab into your cleaning solution and negotiate all those corners.

MAKE IT YOURSELF!

WINDOW CLEANERS

Thoroughly mix 2 tablespoons cornstarch, 1/2 cup ammonia, and 1/2 cup vinegar in a bucket of 3 to 4 quarts warm water. Pour the milky solution into a spray bottle. Spray on windows; wipe with warm water. Rub dry with a paper towel or lint-free cloth.

Here's another window-cleaning solution: Fill a clean, empty spray bottle with 1/2 cup vinegar, 1/4 cup isopropyl rubbing alcohol, and enough water to fill. Spray on windows or glass, and wipe with paper towels.

WINDOW COVERINGS

When you shut the shades to block the view or draw the drapes to hide the windows you didn't have time to wash, you end up looking at smudgy shades or dusty drapes. When light filters through your miniblinds or shutters, eventually the slats appear to be flocked with gray fluff.

Then it's time to do something about your window coverings. As with all the other dirt catchers in your home, regular use of your vacuum cleaner will keep your curtains and blinds from disappearing in a cloud of dust. When more than dust is obscuring your drapes and shutters, we also know what to do.

BLINDS

The best way to clean blinds is to vacuum them regularly with the small-brush attachment of your vacuum cleaner. Close adjustable slats when vacuuming so that you reach more of their surface.

You can remove finger marks with a damp sponge. But when blinds require a thorough cleaning, immerse them in water. Wash them in the bathtub or outdoors by hanging them on the clothesline for scrubbing.

Natural wood blinds with decorative yarn tapes should not be immersed, but plastic, metal, and painted wood blinds can be cleaned in this way.

Pour a low-sudsing, all-purpose cleaner into a bathtub filled with warm water, or for outdoor cleaning mix a solution of ½ cup cleaner in 1 gallon warm water and apply with a brush. If you wear cotton gloves when you wash blinds, you can use your fingers to rub the slats. Rinse the blinds with clean water; allow them to drip-dry either on the clothesline or on the shower-curtain rod, placing towels underneath them to catch drips. Rehang the blinds on the window when the dripping has stopped; stretch the tapes or cords to full length to prevent shrinking. Leave the slats in the open position until the blinds are completely dry.

Put dirty venetian blinds in a tub of warm water; add 1/2 cup baking soda, soak for half an hour, then scrub and rinse.

To prevent dust and pet hair from sticking to window blinds, turn the blinds to the closed position, spray with Static Guard, and let dry.

CURTAINS

Carefully read the care label attached to new curtains, and follow the manufacturer's instructions for cleaning. Using the upholstery attachment on your vacuum cleaner, regularly go over curtain panels for quick cleaning. Vacuuming is almost all the cleaning that fiberglass curtains ever need.

We recommend that you vacuum curtains to remove excess dust before washing. Also disconnect curtain rings and clips (unless they are permanently attached) to prepare your curtains for washing. Fiberglass curtains should be washed and never dry-cleaned. You must wear rubber gloves when hand washing them to protect your hands from glass filaments. Thoroughly rinse the washing machine after washing fiberglass to ensure that no fine glass fragments remain in the tub.

Handle cotton curtains gently if they have been hanging in a sunny window; sunlight may have weakened the fabric. Machine wash sheers, open weave, and other delicate fabrics in a mesh bag or hand wash so that the fabric does not stretch or tear.

Tumble or drip-dry curtains, according to their fabric. Use curtain stretchers for drying lace or net curtains, and iron curtains that need to be pressed before they are completely dry.

DRAPERIES

Draperies are often lined and are usually made of fabrics that are much heavier than those used for curtains. It is usually best to dry-clean draperies, but some drapery fabric is washable.

Dust draperies with the upholstery attachment on your vacuum cleaner. Also vacuum drapes before you wash them or send them out to be cleaned. Don't forget to dust the tops of the drapes, the valances, and the drapery hardware. Occasionally air draperies on a clothesline on a breezy day to refresh them between cleanings.

Remove all hooks and pins unless they are permanently attached before washing or dry-cleaning. If you plan to wash your draperies, test a corner of the fabric in a bowl of warm water and detergent to see if it bleeds. Use only the gentle cycle to wash draperies.

SHADES

Light-diffusing or opaque shades usually are made of fabrics that are washable, and some shades have a protective vinyl coating that makes them very easy to clean. Other shades are not washable and must be dry-cleaned.

Vacuum shades regularly, using the small-brush attachment of your vacuum cleaner. Lower the shades completely before vacuuming to clean the full length. Don't forget the tops of the shades and the valances.

Remove finger marks with a damp sponge or a quick spray of all-purpose cleaner. To thoroughly clean the shades, remove them from the window and spread them out on a flat surface. Test a corner of the shade with a detergent solution to see if the color bleeds.

Make a mild soapsuds solution using a liquid dishwashing detergent, and apply it to a rolled-out shade with a sponge. Rinse with a clean sponge dipped in clear water, and allow the shade to dry before rerolling.

Some spots on nonwashable shades can be removed with an art gum eraser. Use it as though you were erasing a pencil mark. You can also clean grease spots on shades that can't be washed by thoroughly rubbing the surface with a rough, absorbent cloth dipped in cornmeal. The secret of this treatment is that the abrasiveness of the cloth and the absorbency of the cornmeal work together to pick up soil and grease. Terry cloth is good for this job, but an old sweatshirt turned inside out is even better. Dry kitchen flour can be substituted for cornmeal.

SHUTTERS

We recommend that you vacuum all shutters regularly with the small-brush attachment of your vacuum cleaner. Wipe them occasionally with a damp sponge to remove smudges and fingerprints.

For painted shutters, the best care is probably the least, since some polishes and waxes can damage the color and/or decoration. Use warm, soapy water with a damp cloth to wash painted shutters; wash each louver separately on both sides. If you feel you must wax, use a hard paste wax only once a year.

Shutters finished with varnish, lacquer, or wax can be cleaned with commercial aerosol polishing/waxing products. Choose a product that is appropriate for the high-gloss or satin finish of your shutters, but do not spray any cleaner directly onto the shutters because it can seep into the dowels and clog the louvers.

SCREENS

Dip a damp wire brush into baking soda and use it to clean door and window screens. Scrub, then rinse screens with a sponge or a hose.

For spilled popcorn, wayward crumbs, and crunched potato chips, a handheld vacuum will swoosh away the mess in seconds. But eventually you'll have to clean the entire floor. You can rely on an upright vacuum cleaner to clean carpets and rugs quickly and thoroughly.

The easiest way to tackle a large job, like vacuuming a wall-to-wall-carpeted room, is to break it down into sections. When you mow the lawn, you make sure you go over all of it. When you vacuum wall-to-wall carpeting, you can be sure to cover every inch if you divide the floor into quarters. Vacuum an entire quarter before moving on to the next.

It's a good idea to vacuum your rugs and carpets about once a week, or more often in areas of heavy traffic. We're not just talking about hallways and the route to the kitchen. People move their feet around when they sit and grind dirt from their shoes into the carpeting, so you'll need to pay special attention to the carpet in front of chairs and couches, and under desks. Vacuum areas of heavy traffic with a crisscross pattern of overlapping strokes. Every few weeks take a little extra time and use your crevice tool for in-depth cleaning around baseboards and radiators and in other hard-to-reach places.

PREVENTION

* To prevent your family from tracking dirt all over your house, keep a box of baby wipes near the door and have each person clean his or her shoes before entering. (Removing shoes at the door is another excellent practice.)

* A surefire way to cut your cleaning time in half is to put thick mats or throw rugs at all the entrances to your home, both inside and outside the doors. These mats intercept and trap loose dirt, keeping it from being tracked through your house. Compared with cleaning a whole room, throwing a washable rug into the washing machine or vacuuming a doormat takes practically no time at all.

GENERAL CLEANING

* For general cleanup of problem areas on carpets or rugs, use equal parts vinegar and water. Lightly sponge solution into carpet, rinse, and blot dry. Let dry completely.

* To make a carpet and upholstery shampoo, use an eggbeater to mix 1 quart water, 1/4 cup Tide laundry detergent, and 1 tablespoon vinegar. Whip until a stiff foam forms. Gently rub into fabric or carpeting, then remove soiled foam by scraping with a dull knife. Follow with a rinse of clean water.

* A basic cleanser for nongreasy stains: Combine 1/4 teaspoon Dawn dishwashing liquid with 1 cup lukewarm water and blot onto a stain until it's gone. Rinse well and blot with paper towels until dry.

* Try removing grease spots from a rug with a mixture of 1 part salt and 4 parts isopropyl rubbing alcohol. Rub vigorously in the same direction as the nap, then rinse with water. For a larger rug, wipe off the solution with a damp cloth and blot dry. (Protect wood floors by placing several layers of paper towels underneath the rug beforehand.)

REVIVE AND FRESHEN YOUR CARPETS

✳ This treatment will help keep your carpet fresh and clean longer between shampoos: Combine 1/4 cup vinegar and 1 gallon water, then use solution in a steam-cleaning vacuum after shampooing your carpet to remove any residue.

✳ Once a month, sprinkle carpets with baking soda. Let sit overnight, then vacuum.

✳ Revive your carpets by sprinkling cornstarch all over them. Wait 30 minutes, then vacuum and admire the clean.

✳ Mix 1 cup crushed, dried herbs (rosemary, southernwood, lavender, etc.), 1 teaspoon ground cloves, 1 teaspoon ground cinnamon, and 1 teaspoon baking soda. Combine ingredients, and sprinkle over carpet. Let sit for a few minutes, then vacuum.

✳ Mix 1 small box baking soda with a few drops of your favorite essential oil; sprinkle mixture onto carpet. Let sit 10 to 20 minutes, then vacuum.

✳ Use 1 cup baking soda, 1 cup cornstarch, and 15 drops essential oil fragrance. Leave on carpet 10 to 20 minutes, then vacuum. Store mixture in a glass jar or airtight container.

SPECIAL PROBLEMS

If the spot remover you use alters the color of your carpet, try touching up small places with artists' acrylic paint. If that doesn't work, try a felt-tip marker or a permanent-ink marker of the appropriate color. Go slowly and blend the color into the fibers.

To raise depressions left in carpet by heavy furniture, try steaming. Hold a steam iron close enough for steam to reach the carpet, but don't let the iron touch the fibers, especially if they are synthetic, because they could melt. Lift the fibers by scraping them with the edge of a coin or spoon.

If a carpet thread is loose, snip it level with the pile. If you try to pull out the thread, you risk unraveling part of the carpet.

To repair a small area burned down to the carpet backing, snip off the charred fibers, and put white glue in the opening. Then snip fibers from a scrap of carpet or an inconspicuous part of the carpet (perhaps in a closet). When the glue gets tacky, poke the fibers into place. If the burn isn't all the way down to the backing, just snip off the charred tips of the fibers with scissors. The slightly shorter length of a few carpet fibers will never be noticed.

To repair a large burned area in a carpet, cut out the damaged area and substitute a patch of identical size and shape. Secure the new piece of carpeting with double-faced carpet tape or a latex adhesive.

Vacuum History

1869: Ives McGaffey patents a wood-and-canvas "sweeping machine"—the country's first hand-pumped vacuum cleaner—and calls it the Whirlwind.

1901: British engineer Hubert Cecil Booth invents the "vacuum cleaning pump"—a large, horse-drawn wagon containing a gas-powered pump and long hoses.

1908: Department-store janitor James Spangler staples a broom handle to a soapbox, then attaches an old fan motor and a pillowcase; he improves the model and patents the first commercially successful portable electric vacuum cleaner, which comes with a cloth filter bag and attachments.

1922: William Hoover, husband of Spangler's cousin, invests in and becomes president of the sweeper company. He renames it for himself: the Hoover Company.

CARPET STAIN REMOVAL GUIDE

The first rule of carpet cleaning is to wipe up any spill or stain immediately. Often undiluted vinegar can be your best bet for removing a new stain.

This quick-reference guide (in alphabetical order) points to the best cures for the most common carpet spots and stains.

Acid Stains

Acid spills, such as toilet-bowl cleaner, drain cleaner, and vinegar, demand especially quick action. Dilute them immediately with baking soda and water or with club soda. You can tell by feel and smell when the acid spill has been cleaned up. Then apply a solution of ammonia (1 part) and water (10 parts). Rinse with cold water, let dry, and vacuum.

Alcoholic Beverages

If someone spills an alcoholic drink on your carpet, quickly dilute the spot with cold water so that the alcohol does not have time to attack the dyes. Absorb the excess liquid. Then mix 1 teaspoon mild detergent, 1 teaspoon white vinegar, and 1 quart warm water. Apply the solution to the spot. Let the carpet dry. If the spot remains, reapply the solution. Let the carpet dry completely. Vacuum gently.

Blood

Absorb as much of the blood as you can. Then mix 1 teaspoon mild detergent, 1 teaspoon white vinegar, and 1 quart warm water. Apply the solution to the spot. Let the carpet dry. Apply dry-cleaning fluid, and let the carpet dry completely. Vacuum gently.

Butter

The first step in cleaning up a butter spill is to scrape up as much solid butter as you can or to absorb all the melted butter that you can. Apply dry-cleaning fluid. Let the carpet dry. If the spot remains, reapply the fluid, and let the carpet dry thoroughly. Then vacuum.

You can also sprinkle some cornstarch on a butter stain or other greasy spot on your carpet. Let dry completely, then vacuum.

Candle Wax

The easiest way to remove candle wax from your carpet is to press an ice cube against the drip. The wax will harden and can then be pulled off. Treat any remaining traces of wax with dry-cleaning fluid. Let the carpet dry, and vacuum.

Another way to remove candle wax on carpeting is to place a blotter, brown paper bag, or a thick layer of paper towels over the spilled wax, and press with a warm iron until the blotter absorbs the melted wax. Move the blotter frequently so that it doesn't get oversaturated. Remove traces of the wax with spot remover. Let dry, and then vacuum.

Candy

Candy that contains no chocolate is usually easily removed from carpet. Scrape up as much of the candy as you can. Mix 1 teaspoon mild detergent, 1 teaspoon white vinegar, and 1 quart warm water. Apply the solution to the spot. Let the carpet dry. If the spot remains, reapply the solution. Let the carpet dry. Vacuum gently.

Chewing Gum

Chewing gum can be a sticky mess, so harden it by pressing an ice cube against the blob of gum. The gum will harden and can then be pulled off. Treat any remaining traces of the chewing gum with dry-cleaning fluid. Let the carpet dry, and then vacuum.

When chewing gum is stuck in a carpet or rug, put a few ice cubes in a plastic food storage bag and place it directly on the gum. When gum hardens, use a dull knife to scrape it off.

To dissolve chewing gum stuck in carpet or on any cloth, saturate area with vinegar and let it sit briefly. (For faster results, heat vinegar first.) Carefully tug at gum to remove it.

Chocolate

The longer chocolate is allowed to stay on your carpet, the more difficult it is to remove. Scrape the chocolate from the carpet. Mix 1 teaspoon mild detergent, 1 teaspoon white vinegar, and 1 quart warm water. Apply the solution to the spot. Rinse well with clear water, making sure you don't drench the carpet. Let the carpet dry. Vacuum gently.

Clean chocolate stains from carpeting with a mixture of 1 part vinegar and 2 parts water. Sponge on mixture, and blot stain with clean cloths until gone.

Coffee

Blot spilled coffee immediately. Then mix 1 teaspoon mild detergent, 1 teaspoon white vinegar, and 1 quart warm water. Apply the solution to the spot. Let the carpet dry. Apply dry-cleaning fluid, and let the carpet dry again. Vacuum gently.

Clean coffee stains from carpeting with a mixture of 1 part vinegar and 2 parts water. Sponge on mixture, and blot stain with clean cloths until gone.

To remove a coffee or tea stain from a rug or carpet, pour a small amount of beer directly on the spot. Gently rub in the beer with a cloth or a sponge; blot with a paper towel. Repeat until the stain is gone.

Blot up a fresh coffee spill on your carpet with baby wipes—they are absorbent and nongreasy, so they won't add to the stain.

Crayon

Dropped crayons have a knack for getting stepped on and ground into carpeting. Scrape away excess crayon and remove the rest by placing a blotter over the crayon stain and pressing it with a warm iron until the blotter absorbs the melted crayon. Move the blotter frequently so that it doesn't get oversaturated. Apply dry-cleaning fluid, and let the carpet dry. Reapply if necessary, and then vacuum.

Remove crayon stains from carpeting or any other fabric or surface by scrubbing area with a toothbrush dipped in vinegar.

Egg

Like all protein stains, spilled eggs need to be cleaned up immediately. Scrape up as much cooked egg as possible or mop up raw egg. Mix 1 teaspoon mild detergent, 1 teaspoon white vinegar, and 1 quart warm water. Apply the solution to the spot. Let the carpet dry. If the spot remains, reapply the solution. Let the carpet dry. Vacuum gently.

Fruit

Fruit stains can be very hard to remove if they are allowed to set, but if you act quickly this method usually prevents a permanent stain. Scrape up spilled fruit, and absorb fruit juice. Mix 1 teaspoon mild detergent, 1 teaspoon white vinegar, and 1 quart warm water. Apply the solution to the spot. Let the carpet dry. If the spot remains, reapply the solution. Let the carpet dry. Vacuum gently.

Glue

A spot of dried white school glue can be taken out of a carpet with a mixture of 1 part vinegar and 2 parts water. Just sponge on and blot. If the spot is stubborn, cover it with warm vinegar and let it sit for 10 to 15 minutes. When glue has softened, either scrape it up using a dull knife or blot with paper towels.

Gravy

If you accidentally rock the gravy boat, wipe up as much of the spilled gravy as you can. Mix 1 teaspoon mild detergent, 1 teaspoon white vinegar, and 1 quart warm water. Apply the solution to the spot. Let the carpet dry. Apply dry-cleaning fluid. Let the carpet dry. Vacuum gently.

To get rid of a gravy stain on your carpet, first remove as much liquid as possible by covering the spot with salt. This will prevent the greasy stain from spreading. Then follow rug manufacturer's instructions to clean. For this and other stubborn stains, you may need a dry-cleaning solution or an enzyme detergent.

Hand Cream

When you inadvertently squirt hand lotion on your carpet, wipe up the spill immediately. Apply dry-cleaning fluid. Let the carpet dry. If the spot remains, reapply the dry-cleaning fluid. Let the carpet dry, and then vacuum.

Ink

Fast action is essential when you spill ink on carpet. Immediately apply dry-cleaning fluid. Let the carpet dry. If the spot remains, reapply the dry-cleaning fluid. Let the carpet dry thoroughly, and vacuum.

Remove ink stains from carpet with cornstarch. Start with about 2 tablespoons cornstarch, then slowly add enough milk to make a paste. Apply paste, wait a few hours, and brush it off.

Ketchup

Clean ketchup stains from carpeting with a mixture of 1 part vinegar and 2 parts water. Sponge on mixture, and blot stain with clean cloths until gone.

Lipstick

Open tubes of lipstick have a way of falling into the hands of curious toddlers or just falling, period. When your carpet acquires a telltale trace of lipstick, scrape away as much of the lipstick as you can. Apply dry-cleaning fluid, and let it dry; then mix 1 teaspoon mild detergent, 1 teaspoon white vinegar, and 1 quart warm water. Apply the solution to the spot. Let the carpet dry. If the spot remains, reapply the solution. Let the carpet dry. Vacuum gently.

Mildew

The first step in removing mildew stains is to kill the fungus. To do this, mix 1 teaspoon disinfectant cleaner and 1 cup water. Apply the solution to the mildewed carpet, and blot. Then to remove the stain, apply a solution of ammonia (1 part) and water (10 parts). Blot, rinse, and let dry. Vacuum. Keeping the area totally dry is the only way to prevent the reoccurrence of mildew, which can eventually break down carpet fibers.

Milk

Blot up the spilled milk. Mix 1 teaspoon mild detergent, 1 teaspoon white vinegar, and 1 quart warm water. Apply the solution to the spot. Let the carpet dry. Vacuum gently.

Mud

When muddy boots and shoes get past the mats at the entrances to your home, allow the mud tracked onto your carpeting to dry completely, and then brush or scrape off as much as possible. Mix 1 teaspoon mild detergent, 1 teaspoon white vinegar, and 1 quart warm water. Apply the solution to the spot. Let the carpet dry. If the stain remains, apply dry-cleaning fluid and blot dry. When the spot is completely dry, vacuum gently.

Oil

Blot up an oil spill on a rug or carpet right away, then sprinkle baking powder directly on the spot. Let dry, then vacuum up the residue...and the stain!

Nail Polish

Apply dry-cleaning fluid or amyl acetate, acetone, or nail-polish remover to the spilled polish. Test the solvent you plan to use on an inconspicuous part of the carpet. Never apply acetate, acetone, or nail-polish remover to acetate carpet fibers. If the stain remains, mix 1 teaspoon mild detergent, 1 teaspoon white vinegar, and 1 quart warm water. Apply the solution to the spot. Let the carpet dry. Vacuum gently.

Salad Dressing

A misplaced slosh of salad dressing can be removed easily from most carpeting. Absorb as much salad dressing as you can. Mix 1 teaspoon mild detergent, 1 teaspoon white vinegar, and 1 quart warm water. Apply the solution to the spot. Let the carpet dry. If the spot remains, reapply the solution. Let the carpet dry. Vacuum gently.

Salt Deposits

Mix equal amounts of vinegar and water, and use a sponge to apply solution to salt deposits on your rug or carpet. Do not saturate. Let dry, then vacuum.

Soft Drinks

The carbonation in soft drinks will help you clean spilled drinks quickly, but act fast because some of the dyes in the drinks can permanently stain your carpet. Blot up the spilled drink. Mix 1 teaspoon mild detergent, 1 teaspoon white vinegar, and 1 quart warm water. Apply the solution to the spot. Let the carpet dry. If the spot remains, reapply the solution. Let the carpet dry. Vacuum gently.

Clean cola stains from carpeting with a mixture of 1 part vinegar and 2 parts water. Sponge on mixture, and blot stain with clean cloths until gone.

Tar

Remove tar or other stubborn sticky stuff from carpet fibers by rubbing vegetable oil into the substance. Rub the substance loose, then blot with a paper towel.

Tea

The tannic acid in black tea is a potent dye, so move quickly when tea is spilled on your rug. Blot up the tea spill. Mix 1 teaspoon mild detergent, 1 teaspoon white vinegar, and 1 quart warm water. Apply the solution to the spot. Let the carpet dry. Apply dry-cleaning fluid. Let the carpet dry. Vacuum gently.

To remove a coffee or tea stain from a rug or carpet, pour a small amount of beer directly on the spot. Gently rub in the beer with a cloth or a sponge; blot with a paper towel. Repeat until the stain is gone.

Urine

Mix 1 teaspoon mild detergent, 1 teaspoon white vinegar, and 1 quart warm water. Apply the solution to the spot. Let the carpet dry. If the spot remains, reapply the solution. Let the carpet dry. Vacuum gently.

Don't panic when a toddler or your pet has an accident on your carpeting. As soon as you can, blot up as much urine as possible with paper towels, then pour on the club soda. Let sit 1 to 2 minutes and blot again. Repeat if necessary. To remove any last traces, mix equal parts distilled white vinegar and cool water; scrub the solution into the affected area using a stiff brush. Blot up the liquid and rinse with cool water.

Vomit

Treat vomit quickly. Blot up as much as possible, then dilute immediately with baking soda and water or with club soda. Then apply a solution of ammonia (1 part) and water (10 parts). Rinse with cold water, let dry, and then vacuum.

Wine

When red wine is spilled on your carpet, dilute it with white wine, then clean the spot with cold water, and cover with table salt. Wait ten minutes, then vacuum up the salt.

Immediately blot up all moisture from a red wine spill, then sprinkle the area with Morton Salt. Let sit 15 minutes. The salt should absorb any remaining wine in the carpet (turning pink as a result). Clean entire area with a mixture of 1 part white vinegar and 2 parts water.

HARD-SURFACE FLOORS

Unlike other methods of attacking the dirt that piles up on hard-surface floors, using your vacuum cleaner doesn't just push dirt around. Whether it's a handheld vacuum or an upright canister, your vacuum cleaner gets dirt off your hard-surface floors and puts it neatly in a bag so it's ready to be taken out of your home for good.

Vacuuming hard-surface floors before you wash them saves you time because when you wash or polish the floor there is no dirt to grind into the floor covering or turn to mud. To not only speed up cleaning but get your home really clean, always vacuum the floor before you clean it with water or wax.

It is recommended that you vacuum your wood and other hard-surface floors about once a week, more often in areas of heavy traffic or if the floor is dark or very shiny. Lint and dust show up faster on polished surfaces than they do on carpeting, so use a handheld or lightweight cord-less vacuum between regular cleanings to keep your floor sparkling with a minimum of effort. Frequent vacuuming prolongs the life of the floor because it prevents a buildup of grit that can scratch hard-surface flooring.

The techniques you use to vacuum a carpeted room should also be used when you vacuum an uncarpeted room. Vacuum the floor thoroughly, going back and forth across each section. Two slow strokes are usually sufficient to pick up the loose dirt. (Use a small-brush attachment to clean around baseboards and radiators and in other hard-to-reach places.)

There are probably many different kinds of hard-surface floors in your home. Your vacuum cleaner can help you maintain all the floors in your home, from the concrete in your basement to the parquet under the rug in the living room. Unfortunately, weekly vacuuming is not all it takes to keep a hard-surface floor looking its best. So here are a few quick and easy cleaning methods to help you speed through the heel marks and the sticky stuff that accumulate on your hard-surface floors.

Whenever you go to the grocery or hardware store, you will find an array of specialized cleaning products. Many commercial products are very good at cleaning what they are designed to clean. Which products you use to clean your floors is entirely up to you. We have included some tried-and-true recipes for cleaners that can be made from products you're likely to have in your cupboards. These solutions and methods don't necessarily work better than commercial products, but they all work as well. So if you have time to clean your bathroom floor, but you've run out of the cleaner you usually use, try the homemade remedy. It will save you money, and it will save you time, since you won't have to run out to the store before you start to clean.

What's in household dust? It's composed of fibers from textiles and plants. It also may contain human skin flakes, pet dander, bits of insects and other bugs, pollen, household insulation, and carpet backing.

GENERAL

To prevent scratching the floor when moving heavy furniture across uncarpeted areas, slip scraps of carpeting, pile down, under the furniture legs.

ASPHALT TILE

An asphalt-tile floor won't retain leg imprints when you replace your old favorite TV chair in the family room with a snazzy new one. But even though asphalt tile recovers well from indentations, we suggest that you use plastic, not rubber, casters and cups on furniture legs to minimize scratches and indentations. Although asphalt is resilient, you should know that grease, oil, and solvents—such as kerosene, gasoline, naphtha, and turpentine—or harsh cleaning preparations and strong soaps as well as scouring can leave the surface of your floor looking like the moon.

If you take the time to damp mop your asphalt floor every week, you will not have to wash and polish it as often as if you allow dirt to build up. But make sure that the cleaner/polish you use can withstand damp mopping. If it can't, you will have to reapply it. We've found that adding a cup of fabric softener to a half pail of water will prevent damp mopping from dulling the shine on your floor.

When you decide to wash the floor, don't flood the floor with water; excess water can seep into the seams and loosen adhesives that hold down the flooring.

MAKE IT YOURSELF!

ASPHALT CLEANERS

Mix 1/4 cup low-sudsing, all-purpose cleaner; 1 cup ammonia; and 1/2 gallon cool or cold water. **Caution:** Wear rubber gloves, and work in a well-ventilated area when using this powerful solution. Apply the cleaner to the floor with a sponge mop, using pressure for heavily soiled areas. Rinse with cool, clear water for spotless results. Apply two thin coats of a water-based, self-polishing floor finish, allowing the floor to dry between coats.

Mix ½ cup vinegar, 2 tablespoons furniture polish, and 1 gallon warm water. **Caution:** Wear rubber gloves. Mop the floor with this mixture, using a sponge mop or string mop.

BRICK

Your brick floor may appear to be very durable because of its hard, fired surface. But in reality brick is porous and stains easily. For this reason, the best way to care for your brick floor is to keep it sealed and waxed. You'll need to use a commercial sealer for brick.

Damp mopping with a sponge mop or string mop after vacuuming will prevent dirt from building up on your brick floor, so you can put off washing and/or stripping the floor. Try adding a cup of vinegar to the mop water; the floor will glisten without being polished—a real time-saver.

If you use a water-based, self-polishing liquid wax, you'll occasionally have to strip the wax buildup before you rewax. Use a solvent-based wax so that you don't have to strip your floor. A solvent-based polish can be applied over a water-based polish, but a water-based polish cannot be applied over a solvent-based polish. The solvents in the wax dissolve the layer of wax that is on the floor every time solvent-based wax is applied, so there is no wax buildup.

If your floor has a wax buildup, you can remove it by applying a wax-stripping product with a scrub brush or floor-scrubbing machine that has a brush attachment. Rinse the floor thoroughly with clear water after applying the stripper according to the manufacturer's directions. Do not clean your brick floor with acids, strong soaps, or abrasives.

Caring for a porous brick floor is a lot of work no matter what you do. If you use a solvent-based wax on the floor, you have to seal it. If you use a water-based polish, you'll occasionally have to strip the wax buildup.

While the following method of caring for a brick floor is not as effective as a treatment with stripper, sealer, and paste wax, it is a quick and inexpensive way to take care of your brick floor. Since this homemade solution contains ammonia, you strip the floor every time you wash it, eliminating wax buildup. Most acrylic liquid waxes are self-sealing, allowing you to skip the application of a sealer.

Clean and strip the floor with a solution of ¼ cup low-sudsing, all-purpose cleaner; 1 cup clear ammonia; and ½ gallon cool or cold water. **Caution:** Wear rubber gloves, and work in a well-ventilated area when using this powerful solution. Apply the solution to the floor with a sponge mop, using pressure for heavily soiled areas; rinse with cool, clear water for spotless results. Then apply two thin coats of an acrylic floor wax.

CONCRETE

If you're like most people, you probably put off dealing with the concrete floors in your unfinished basement and garage for as long as possible. The result is that they get really dirty because concrete is very porous and soaks up stains quickly. While few of us are so fastidious as to seal or paint our garage floors, the time you take to seal a basement floor, especially if it is new, will save time in the long run, since the sealed floor will require little more cleaning than vacuuming. When your basement floor does have to be washed, go ahead and get it really clean by washing it with a strong, all-purpose cleaning solution.

Mix ¼ cup low-sudsing, all-purpose cleaner; 1 cup clear ammonia; and ½ gallon cool or cold water. **Caution:** Wear rubber gloves, and work in a well-ventilated area when using this powerful solution. Apply to the concrete floor with a sponge mop, using pressure for heavily soiled areas; rinse with cool, clear water for spotless results. Let the floor dry.

CORK

A cork floor recovers quickly from the pressure of chair legs and the wear and tear of heavy foot traffic, but water will do it in every time; even the small amount of H2O in water-based cleaners is too much wet for a cork floor. You must use only solvent-based cleaners and polishes to maintain cork-tile flooring.

A new cork floor should be sealed with varnish, shellac, or lacquer. Paint or lacquer thinner, alcohol, and other chemicals will damage these sealers, so try not to use them near the floor.

You can remove heel marks from your cork floor by applying a solvent-based wax, polish, or cleaner to a rag and rubbing the mark.

The fastest way to clean a cork floor is with a one-step product specifically formulated to clean and polish cork floors. Unfortunately, the fastest way is not the best way to care for cork. If your floor is new or a focal point of your home, you should take the time twice a year to clean the floor with a liquid wood-floor cleaning product and to rewax. Use a liquid cleaner/wax that soaks into the floor. Wipe up the excess liquid, and allow the floor to dry, then buff it with a floor polisher.

The second step of this process is to apply a liquid or paste solvent-based wax. No stripping will ever be necessary because the solvents in the new wax will strip off the old wax. Shake solvent-based liquid polishes vigorously before use. All you have to do to renew the shine between cleanings is to buff the floor when it appears dull.

FLAGSTONE & SLATE

These natural-stone flooring materials are similar in that they have rough, porous surfaces and are set into grout. This type of flooring wears like rock, but it will look like it should have been left outside if it is not cared for properly. Flagstone and slate floors must be sealed with a commercial sealer, not lacquer or varnish.

The best way to seal a flagstone or slate floor is with a sealer for terrazzo and slate. After the sealer dries, apply two thin coats of an acrylic floor finish with a long-handled wax applicator fitted with a lamb's wool pad, or apply paste wax with a floor-polishing machine. To do this, use a spatula to spread a small amount of paste wax directly on the brushes of the polisher. Slowly operate the polisher back and forth to apply an even, thin coat of wax. When dry, buff the floor.

A self-polishing liquid will build up on your floor, and you'll occasionally have to strip the wax buildup and rewax. Applying a wax-stripping product with a floor-scrubbing machine that has a brush attachment will keep you off your knees, but if you don't have a machine, a scrub brush will work. After applying the stripper according to the manufacturer's directions, rinse the floor thoroughly with clear water. Then apply wax to the floor.

To keep ahead of dirt, damp mop flagstone or slate floors with a sponge mop or string mop, using clear water, an all-purpose cleaning solution in warm water, or water to which fabric softener has been added. Wring the mop until it doesn't drip, and apply it to the floor in slow, even strokes with just enough pressure to loosen and pick up dirt. If the freshly mopped floor dries with a luster-dulling film, you can mop it again with water containing a cup of white vinegar; the floor will glisten.

Mix ¼ cup low-sudsing, all-purpose cleaner; 1 cup clear ammonia; and ½ gallon cool or cold water. **Caution:** Wear rubber gloves, and work in a well-ventilated area when using this powerful solution. Apply to the floor with a sponge mop, using pressure for heavily soiled areas. Rinse the floor thoroughly with clean water. Apply sealer, then buff.

LINOLEUM

Sad but true, linoleum must be waxed to shine and stand up to foot traffic effectively. But once it is waxed, the only regular maintenance a linoleum floor needs is vacuuming and an occasional swipe with a damp mop. A cup of vinegar in the mop water will bring up the shine on the floor, so you can delay rewaxing until it's really necessary.

Remove heel marks from linoleum by dipping fine-grade (000) steel wool in liquid floor wax. Rub the spot gently, and wipe with a damp cloth.

A water-based cleaner/polish or an all-purpose cleaning solution is best for the routine care of a linoleum floor. Solvent-based products can soften and damage linoleum. Scouring the floor, flooding it with water, or using very hot water or strong soaps are other no-nos for taking care of linoleum floors.

The fastest way to clean a linoleum floor is with a one-step cleaner/polish, but the best way to clean the floor is to mop it with an all-purpose cleaner. Dissolve the cleaner in very warm water, rinse, and apply two thin coats (let dry between coats) of a water-based, self-polishing liquid. Use a long-handled wax applicator fitted with a washable chenille pad.

Occasionally, you'll have to remove wax buildup with an all-purpose cleaner or stripper. We recommend that you always test a corner of the floor before stripping the whole thing to make sure the product you're using won't permanently damage the flooring.

* Scrub a linoleum floor with a mixture of 1 gallon water and 1 cup vinegar. If floor needs a polish after this, use straight club soda.
* Mop up salt deposits from winter boots with a mixture of equal parts vinegar and water.
* Mix 1/2 cup vinegar, 2 tablespoons furniture polish, and 1 gallon cool or cold water. Mop the floor with this mixture, using a sponge or string mop.
* Sometimes you can flatten bulges or curled seams in a linoleum floor by placing aluminum foil over them and ironing them with your iron. (The heat will soften and reactivate the adhesive.) Position weights, such as stacks of books, over treated areas to keep them flat until the adhesive cools and hardens.

MARBLE

Marble flooring is becoming more and more popular for almost every room in the house; it's available in a variety of colors, with a polished or nonpolished finish, and in an array of new thicknesses and shapes. Nonpolished marble is very porous, stains easily, and must be sealed with a commercial sealer. Don't use varnish or lacquer to seal marble; it quickly peels off. Polished marble is less porous but can still be stained; we recommend a commercial marble sealer for this finish also.

Marble floors look great after being damp mopped with a sponge mop or string mop, using clear water, an all-purpose cleaning solution in warm water, or a mixture of 1 cup fabric softener and ½ gallon water. Wring the mop until it doesn't drip, and apply the mixture to the floor in slow, even strokes with just enough pressure to loosen and pick up dirt. If the mopped floor dries with a luster-dulling film, mop it again with water containing a cup of white vinegar. The floor will glisten—it sure beats rewaxing.

Water-based, self-polishing liquid wax is a fast, shiny finish for marble. There's only one problem with using it (and it's a big one): Occasionally, you'll have to strip the wax buildup and rewax.

Applying a wax-stripping product with a floor-scrubbing machine with a brush attachment makes the job slightly more pleasant than crawling around on your knees with a scrub brush. After applying the stripper according to the manufacturer's directions, rinse the floor thoroughly with clear water. Then apply wax to the floor.

You can use either a water-based self-polishing wax or a paste wax. If you use a water-based polish, don't shake it before use. A solvent-based polish can be applied over a water-based polish, but a water-based polish cannot be applied over a solvent-based polish. If you use a paste wax, test it in a comer to see if it will discolor the flooring. If a solvent-based paste wax is used, rewax to strip the old wax and to renew the shine.

RUBBER TILE

Rubber tile is slightly delicate; it can be damaged by exposure to direct sunlight, and it is easily wrecked by strong cleaners. Care for rubber tile in much the same way that you maintain asphalt tile, but you'll have to be a little more careful.

No one has time to wash floors on a weekly basis, but most of us can find time to pass a damp mop over the floor after we've vacuumed it. This will delay for a long time the day when you finally have to mop. A trick we've found to make a rubber-tile floor look freshly waxed is to add a cup of fabric softener to a half pail of water. This prevents damp mopping from dulling the shine on your floor. Also, be sure that you use a cleaner/polish that can withstand damp mopping; if it can't, you'll end up reapplying the cleaner/polish every time you mop.

The quickest way we have found to clean a rubber-tile floor is to use a water-based cleaner/polish or an all-purpose cleaning solution. It is recommended that you read the product label for precautionary measures and test any cleaner in a corner before using it on the entire floor.

Occasionally, remove wax buildup with a cleaner or wax stripper. Follow stripping with two thin coats of self-polishing wax; allow to dry between coats. Two thin coats make a much more durable, long-lasting finish than one coat, which may dry slowly and leave a gummy, dust-collecting mess on your floor.

Remove heel marks from rubber tile by dipping fine-grade (000) steel wool in liquid floor wax. Rub the spot gently, and wipe with a damp cloth.

Solvent-based products can soften and damage a rubber-tile floor. Also, keep scouring pads, strong soaps, and hot water away from rubber tile.

Flooding the floor with water will also cause big problems; excess water can seep into the seams and loosen the adhesives that hold down the flooring.

MAKE IT YOURSELF!

CLEANER/POLISH FOR RUBBER TILE

Mix ½ cup vinegar, 2 tablespoons furniture polish, and 1 gallon warm water. **Caution:** Wear rubber gloves. Mop the floor with this mixture, using a sponge or string mop.

TILE

✳   Clean tile floors with 1/2 cup baking soda in a bucket of warm water. Mop and rinse clean.

✳   Make ceramic tile floors shine by mopping with a mixture of 1 cup vinegar and 1 gallon warm water.

✳   Add extra shine to your clean, dry tile floor. Wrap a piece of wax paper around a dust mop and sweep it over the floor.

✳   Wash grout between terra-cotta tiles with straight vinegar to clean up and prevent smudges.

* WD-40 can remove the following (and likely many more things) from tile floors: scuff marks, mascara, gum, coffee stains, crayon, ink, marker, adhesives, rubber cement, and glue.

* To remove a floor tile for replacement, lay a piece of aluminum foil on it and then press down with your iron set at medium. The heat of the iron will soften the tile's adhesive, and you can easily pry up the tile with a putty knife or scraper.

* To remove a damaged floor tile, soften it with a propane torch fitted with a flame-spreader nozzle. (Be careful not to damage surrounding tiles.) When the tile is soft, pry it up with a putty knife and scrape the old adhesive off the subfloor so that the replacement tile will bond cleanly.

* You can remove a floor tile by covering it with dry ice. Wear work gloves to protect your hands. Let the dry ice stand for ten minutes. The cold will make the tile brittle, so it will shatter easily. Chisel out the tile from the edges to the center.

* Laying floor tile will be easier if the room temperature is at least 70 degrees Fahrenheit before you start, because tile is more pliable at higher temperatures. Put all boxes of tile in the room for at least 24 hours prior to positioning tiles on the floor. Try to keep the room temperature at the same level for about a week after laying the tiles, and then wait at least a week before washing the floor.

* After laying floor tiles, you can help them lie flat by going over them with a rolling pin.

VINYL

Vinyl floor coverings are ideal for everyone who hates to clean. They are truly easy-care, and there are many excellent products on the market that are designed to maintain a sparkling vinyl floor in one quick step.

If you don't want to use one of these products, the best way to clean a vinyl-tile floor is with an all-purpose cleaner dissolved in water. After you have cleaned the floor, rinse the tile with clear water to make sure no film remains to dull the finish. When the floor is dry, apply two thin coats of water-based, self-polishing floor finish, allowing the floor to dry between coats. Apply the wax with a long-handled wax applicator fitted with a washable chenille pad.

It will be a long time before you need to do anything more for your floor than to wipe up spills and vacuum. But if you want to damp mop after vacuuming, add a cup of fabric softener to a half pail of water to prevent damp mopping from dulling the shine on your vinyl floor.

Remove heel marks from vinyl floors by dipping a synthetic scouring pad in liquid floor wax. Rub the spot gently and wipe with a damp cloth.

MAKE IT YOURSELF!

CLEANER/POLISH FOR VINYL

Mix ½ cup vinegar, 2 tablespoons furniture polish, and 1 gallon warm water. **Caution:** Wear rubber gloves. Mop the floor with this mixture, using a sponge or string mop.

VINYL, "NO-WAX"

A "no-wax" vinyl floor is a breeze to maintain. All you have to do is keep it clean, and damp mopping after vacuuming goes a long way toward doing that. Obviously, you don't have time to mop the kitchen floor after dinner every day, so go ahead and wipe up spills with a sponge dipped in dishwashing liquid, scrub off heel marks with a synthetic scouring pad, and put off washing the floor until it gets really sticky, if you want to.

When it's finally time to wash the floor, use an all-purpose cleaning solution. Always be sure to read the product label for precautionary measures and instructions. Test any cleaner in a corner before using it on the entire floor. Sometimes a "no-wax" floor dries with a luster-dulling film; don't panic, just mop it again with water containing a cup of white vinegar, and the floor will glisten like new.

If your "no-wax" floor loses its shine in high-traffic areas, use a gloss-renewing product available from the manufacturer of your floor or another commercial product designed for this purpose. Never throw just anything you have around the house on the dull floor: Solvent-based products or cleaners that contain pine oil can soften and permanently damage a vinyl-tile floor. Also, do not scour "no-wax" vinyl, use strong soaps and hot water, or flood the floor with water. Excess water can seep into the seams and loosen the adhesives that hold down the flooring.

WOOD FLOORS

There is almost nothing as elegant as a glimmering wood floor. The sight of such a floor speaks to us of glamour, good living, and a lot of very hard work on somebody's part (preferably not yours). It's true that you have to take care of a wood floor, but you don't have to break your back to do it if you care for it our way.

The product used to seal a wood floor determines how it can be cared for. Varnish, shellac, poly-urethane, and lacquer are used to finish floors, but only polyurethane requires no further treat-ment, including waxing. The integrity and beauty of wood floors not finished with polyurethane can be maintained only by using solvent-based cleaners and polishes. Water should never be used on wood floors, except those treated with polyurethane; these can be damp mopped. If you have the choice and don't want to spend your time maintaining your wood floor, we recommend that you have your wood floors finished with polyurethane.

For those of you who have lacquered, varnished, or shellacked floors, the fastest way to clean a wood floor is with a one-step cleaner/polish. After vacuuming the floor, pour the solvent-based liquid on a small area and rub lightly with a clean, dry wax applicator. Working on a small section at a time, stroke the floor in the direction of the grain. Blot up any excess liquid with a clean cloth.

As it sometimes happens, the best way to clean a wood floor is not the fastest; so if you want a long-lasting shine on your wood floor, you will have to spend more time and follow this tested method. After vacuuming the floor, apply a liquid wood-floor cleaner with a dry wax applicator or a cloth on a small area at a time. Let it soak for 3 minutes, and wipe up the excess.

When the floor is dry, buff with a floor polisher. **Caution:** This is a combustible mixture; use in a well-ventilated area.

Unless you always take off your shoes at the door, you'll probably have to apply a liquid or paste solvent-based wax to your wood floor about twice a year. No stripping is necessary because the solvents in the new wax will strip off the old wax. Make sure the room is well ventilated when using solvent-based waxes and polishes.

Here are a few more tips for maintaining your floors:

* If your wood floors are clean but a bit dull, mop cooled Lipton tea over them. Let them air-dry, then buff to a shine with a clean towel.
* To polish a varnished wood floor, put a folded bath towel into one leg of a pair of pantyhose and start buffing!
* Remove water spots on wood floors with a sponge dampened in a solution of 4 table spoons baking soda and 1 quart warm water.
* To remove chewing gum stuck to a hardwood floor, set a food storage of ice cubes atop the gum. After gum hardens, use an old credit card to pry it loose. If necessary, polish that area of the floor after gum is removed.
* Add 1 cup vinegar to 1 gallon of water; mop lightly onto hardwood floors (do not saturate). No need to rinse. This will keep floors shiny and remove any greasy buildup.
* If you have a squeaky wood floor under tile or carpet, you may be able to eliminate the squeak without removing the floor covering. Try to reset loose boards by pounding a hammer on a block of scrap wood in the area over the squeaky boards. The pressure may force loose nails back into place.
* You may be able to silence a squeaky wood floor by using talcum powder as a dry lubricant. Sprinkle powder over the offending areas, and sweep it back and forth until it filters down between the cracks.
* Try filling dents in a wood floor with clear nail polish or shellac. Because the floor's color will show through, the dents will not be apparent.

FURNITURE

If your home is like most, much of your furniture probably does all kinds of things it wasn't intended to do. The upholstered chair by the front door is a catchall for schoolbooks and jackets. The dining table doubles as a sewing table, desk, or computer center. And many of us practically live in bed, snacking, reading, watching TV, or just recovering from the day at work. Grime builds up on the chair, lint sticks to the dining table, and cracker crumbs work their way into the mattress. We've found that you can maintain (or restore) the good looks of most furniture with the proper care.

WOOD FURNITURE

* To remove dirt, grime, and built-up polish from wood furniture, brew some tea. Steep 2 Lipton Tea Bags in 4 cups boiling water; let cool. Dampen a soft, clean cloth with tea and wipe down the dirty surfaces. Polish with a soft, clean cloth.
* Beer: It's not just for stacking in pyramids on the coffee table. Clean wood furniture, especially oak and mahogany, with warm beer. (It's okay if it's stale.) Using a clean, soft cloth, wipe it on the wood; wipe dry with a second cloth.
* To remove a surface mark from a wood table, whether a water mark or a scald from a hot dish, make a thin paste of vegetable oil and a pinch of salt. (Use about 1/8 to 1/4 teaspoon salt per tablespoon of oil.) Just wipe on paste with a soft cloth, then buff lightly as you wipe it off.
* Apply mayonnaise to white rings, spots, or crayon marks on your wood furniture, let it sit for 1 hour, then wipe clean with a soft cloth or sponge.
* Remove paper that's stuck on a wood surface by generously applying cooking spray. Wait 5 to 10 minutes, then carefully remove the paper.
* Dusting carved wood furniture can be difficult. Use a Q-tips cotton swab for the small spaces. Additionally, a swab dipped in furniture polish is a great tool for shining and protecting your beautiful furniture.

* Remove waxy buildup on wood tabletops with a solution of equal parts water and vinegar. Wipe onto area, then rub and dry immediately using a soft cloth.
* To restore luster to mahogany furniture, mix 3 tablespoons vinegar and 1 quart water. Dip a sponge in the mixture, wring thoroughly, then use to wipe wood. Do not saturate.
* After polishing any wood furniture in your home, sprinkle a bit of cornstarch over the surface. Then use a clean, soft cloth to buff it to a high shine. Any excess oil will be absorbed by the cornstarch.
* If the old wood boards you acquired have great potential (and a great amount of grime), try this cleanser. Mix 3 parts sand, 2 parts Ivory Liquid Hand Cleanser, and 1 part lime juice thoroughly in a bucket. Using a stiff brush, scrub the wood with the cleanser. Rinse with water; rub dry with a clean towel. Now get on with making that furniture!

MAKE IT YOURSELF!

WOOD POLISHES

Try this recipe for homemade furniture polish. Whisk 1/2 teaspoon extra virgin olive oil and 1/4 cup white vinegar in a small bowl. Pour mixture into a clean, resealable jar and label clearly. When ready to use, give jar a good shake, then apply polish liberally to wood surfaces with a soft cloth. Wipe away excess.

Here's another homemade polish for general use on all wood furniture. In a glass jar with a tight-fitting lid, mix 1/4 cup fresh or store-bought lemon juice with 1/2 cup vegetable oil. Apply to wood furniture with a cotton cloth, rubbing in a small amount at a time. Kept out of direct sunlight, this mixture can be stored for several months.

To remove scratches from a wood table, increase the amount of lemon juice in the previous furniture polish recipe so that you're using equal parts lemon juice and vegetable oil. With a soft, clean cotton cloth, gently rub the mixture into the wood, buffing out the scratches. Repeat as needed until scratches are gone.

UPHOLSTERED FURNITURE

* Turn the cushions on your chairs and sofas regularly to ensure even wear on the furniture.

* Shampoo or deep-clean upholstered furniture when vacuuming and spot cleaning fail to make it look fresh.

* Most furniture upholstered in fabric can be shampooed safely at home; the exception to this is fabric marked "dry-clean only." But you can spot clean this kind of fabric with a solvent-based cleaner.

* Many commercial fabric shampoos are available. If you use one, be sure to read the manufacturer's instructions.

* Upholstered furniture should not be placed in constant, direct sunlight or near heating outlets; this can cause fading or discoloration.

* To remove spilled grease from upholstery, cover the spot right away with cornstarch. Wait until as much of the grease as possible has been absorbed, then vacuum. Repeat if necessary.

* To remove an oily stain from upholstered furniture, grind about a cup of cat litter into a powder and scatter it over the stain. Wait until the oil is absorbed, then vacuum up the litter.

* A fresh grease stain on a cloth chair can be absorbed with equal parts baking soda and salt. Sprinkle the mixture onto the stain and rub lightly; leave on for a few hours, then vacuum.

* A trick for removing lint and pet hair from upholstery is to rub the fabric with a dryer sheet.

- Pick up pet hair easily by wrapping your hand with a piece of duct tape with the sticky side out. Run your hand along the upholstery and pick up the hair.

UPHOLSTERY SHAMPOO

Mix ¼ cup dishwashing liquid with 1 cup warm water and whip the solution with an eggbeater. Apply the foam to the upholstery, a small section at a time, with a soft-bristled brush. Shake off any excess water. Rinse the upholstery by gently rubbing the fabric with a moist, clean cloth; rinse the cloth as necessary.

LEATHER

Leather must be cleaned with pure soap products (no detergents) and benefits from occasional applications of conditioner to restore moisture and bring up the sheen.

- Keep a leather armchair looking like new. Every few weeks, wipe it with a soft cotton cloth that's been dipped in beaten egg white. Buff to a shine with a second cloth.
- To keep leather upholstery looking its best, give it a milk bath. Every 3 months, use a clean cloth to wipe on a small quantity of skim milk.
- A sudsy solution of soap flakes and warm water is a good way to clean leather upholstery. Apply the suds only, scrubbing gently with a soft-bristled brush; wipe clean with a damp sponge.

VINYL

- Clean vinyl upholstery, such as that on a recliner or kitchen chair, with a paste of baking soda and water. Rub on, allow to dry, then wipe off.

* Clean up spots on vinyl furniture by wiping with a cloth dipped in undiluted vinegar.

* Erase ink stains from vinyl surfaces by rubbing on a bit of vegetable shortening with a cloth or paper towel. Use a little elbow grease and scrub until stains disappear. Wipe clean with a fresh towel.

GLASS

To bring out the shine in a glass tabletop, rub it gently with a few drops of lemon juice. Dry with a paper towel, then polish with a piece of crumpled-up newspaper.

WICKER AND CANE

Prevent white wicker furniture from yellowing by scrubbing it with a stiff brush moistened with salt water. Let dry in full sunlight.

Clean cane furniture with baking powder. Wet the cane with warm water, then apply the powder with a paintbrush. Let dry; brush off. Rinse with cold water and allow to air-dry.

FANS

After cleaning the blades of a fan (any kind: freestanding, oscillating, or ceiling fan), wipe the surfaces with a dryer sheet. This will slow the accumulation of hair, dust, and dirt.

LAMP SHADES

Since many lamp shades direct a beam light onto their collected cobwebs and dust, they'll need to be cleaned more frequently than less-obvious dirt collectors. Lamp shades are made of many different materials. Some are washable and some are not; keep all the care information from the manufacturer so you know the proper cleaning procedure for your lamp shade.

Remove dust and cobwebs from lamp shades with the small-brush attachment of your vacuum cleaner.

Wash silk, nylon, and rayon shades only if they are sewn onto their frame. Dry-clean shades that are glued to their frames. Remove spots from nonwashable fabric shades with spot remover.

We recommend that you use your bathtub or a large laundry sink to wash lamp shades. Make a sudsy warm-water solution with liquid dishwashing detergent. Dip the shade in and out of the solution, making sure that the shade is completely covered, and then rinse it in lukewarm water, following the same dipping procedure. Rinse until the water is clear. Take the shade outside and swing it vigorously in a circle to get rid of excess moisture, and then dry it in the sun or with an electric fan or hair dryer.

If your lamp shade is washable but has glued-on trim that prevents you from immersing it in water, use the following method for cleaning:

 MAKE IT YOURSELF! **LAMP-SHADE CLEANER**

Mix ¼ cup dishwashing liquid with 1 cup warm water and whip the mixture with an eggbeater until it makes a stiff foam. Apply the foam to the shade with a sponge, being careful not to wet the trim. Rinse by going over the shade with a clean cloth wrung out in clear water. Allow the shade to dry.

SLIPCOVERS

Slipcovers usually are washable. Refer to the manufacturer's care instructions or the fabric-care label for cleaning information.

Use your vacuum cleaner to remove lint and dust from slipcovers before washing them. Mend any ripped seams, close all zippers and fasteners, and pretreat heavy soil and spots before washing them.

Machine wash slipcovers whenever possible. Hand washing is suitable only for small pieces. Select the appropriate water temperature for the fabric, but never use hot water if there is any possibility of shrinking or fading.

Machine-dry the slipcover until it is slightly damp, not completely dry. Press pleats or ruffles if necessary before refitting the slipcover on the furniture. Put a slipcover back on the furniture while it is still damp for a smooth fit.

CHOOSING FURNITURE

* It's risky to buy furniture off the back of a truck. The price—and the sample on view—may be attractive, and the cartons may even bear a good brand name, but by the time you find out that the boxed furniture is of inferior quality the truck and driver will be long gone.

* Furniture items advertised for sale "as is" sometimes provide wonderful bargains, but you should be sure to identify the damage before the purchase. A minor scratch may be something you can live with (or fix yourself), but avoid structural damage unless you're willing to pay for repairs.

* Good furniture bargains are available at close-out sales, but be sure you won't want to match the piece later. A "close out" is a style the manufacturer is discontinuing, and you will not be able to find replacements or additions once the consignment is gone.

* Look for levelers, mechanical devices built into the furniture's base that compensate for uneven floors, when you buy tall pieces of furniture such as china cabinets and wall units.

* The fabric on the arms of upholstered chairs and sofas will wear twice as long if the piece comes with matching arm caps.

* Zippered sofa cushions should not be removed for cleaning or washing. Clean them according to the manufacturer's directions while they are on the cushion.

* Vinyl-covered furniture may be a good choice for a family room or high-traffic area, but it's not invulnerable. Body oils and perspiration can harden vinyl, and tears are difficult to repair. Keep this in mind when making your choice.

* Lightweight fabrics wear better when they are quilted; the quilting allows the fabric to stretch under stress.

* The fabric used to upholster a piece of furniture can boost the price to a surprising degree. If you suspect that a piece you like owes its price to a lush fabric, ask if the piece is available with a less expensive covering.

* A fabric that has the design woven in is likely to be more serviceable than one that is printed only on one side.

* If your household is particularly hard on furniture—or if you have cats—keep in mind that nubby fabrics are more likely to snag and pill than smooth ones.

* There's more to upholstered furniture than meets the eye, so check the frame that supports it. Lift one end of the piece; it shouldn't wobble or creak. If it does, the construction may be inferior.

* Push hard on the arms and back of an upholstered chair. You shouldn't be able to feel hard frame edges through the fabric. If you can, the chair is poorly padded and will wear out quickly.

* Before you go shopping for furniture, make a floor plan of your room. Use grid paper and a scale of one square on the grid to one square foot of floor space. Mark in doors, windows, heating outlets, electrical outlets, and other features that will influence where you can and cannot position a piece of furniture. That way you'll avoid buying a bookcase that blocks your most conveniently placed electrical outlets, or a sofa that has to sit on top of your floor heating duct. Take your floor plan and tape measure when you shop – a chair that looks quite small on the showroom floor may look a lot bigger when you get it into your living room.

* If you move frequently, be wary of buying furniture with a specific location in mind. Look instead for items that are adaptable to many spaces and uses.

* When buying furniture, comfort should be near the top of your list of criteria. You'll grow tired of even the most elegant chair if it's not comfortable to relax in.

* It's a good idea to visit department and furniture stores that display furniture in room-style groupings. It's sometimes much easier to imagine how furniture will look in your own home if you see it in a homelike setting.

* When selecting furniture, consider the traffic patterns of your home. That handsome coffee table that looks so good on the showroom floor will be a lot less attractive if it's going to block everyone's route to the kitchen or the stairs.

* Fold a printed fabric and rub the printed sides together. If any of the print comes off, don't buy the fabric. It's an inferior product.

* Tightly woven fabrics wear better than loosely woven ones. To check the weave, hold the fabric up to the light. Spots of light will show through a loose weave.

DECORATIVE ITEMS

Your prize possession may be a collection of pewter salt-and-pepper shakers depicting national monuments or the box of bone-handled knives your brother gave you on your birthday. The decorative objects you've collected and cherish add visual interest to your home and sometimes become treasured family heirlooms. They'll also need to be cleaned from time to time. Most of your things can be safely cared for at home, especially if frequent dusting has kept dirt from building up on their surfaces.

PIANOS

* Restore yellowed piano keys to their original shine with mayonnaise or vinegar. Rub on a small amount with a soft, dry cloth; wipe clean with a damp cloth. Do not saturate. Polish to a shine with another dry cloth.

* Bring back the shine on piano keys and gilt picture frames by rubbing carefully with a cloth dipped in milk.

* To clean and remove stickers from the keys of pianos and synthesizers, all it takes is a little WD-40 and a clean cloth.

MIRRORS

* Make your mirrors shine by washing them with a bucket of water combined with 1 tablespoon ammonia.

* Your mirror will sparkle after this tea break. Brew a pot of strong Lipton tea; let cool. Dip a soft cloth into the tea, then wipe it over the whole mirror. Buff with a soft, dry cloth.

METALS: SILVER, BRASS, COPPER, & PEWTER

* To remove silver tarnish using a process called ion exchange, boil a pot of water and 1/2 teaspoon salt with 1 to 2 teaspoons baking soda. Place the tarnished pieces of silverware in a pan with the saltwater solution along with a piece of aluminum foil. Soak for 2 to 3 minutes. Rinse the silverware well, then use a soft cloth to buff dry.

* Clean and polish your precious metals with chalk. Sprinkle a little powdered chalk onto a clean, damp cloth. Rub a tarnished piece until shiny. Rinse with water; dry.

* To remove salt stains from a silver saltshaker or another silver piece, rub with extra virgin olive oil. Let sit a few days, then wipe with a clean cotton cloth.

* Because pewter is a soft metal that can be damaged easily, it must be cleaned gently. Add enough all-purpose flour to a mixture of 1 teaspoon salt and 1 cup distilled white vinegar to make a smooth paste. Apply paste to a pewter piece with a soft cloth. Let dry (about half an hour); rinse with warm water. Polish with a soft cloth, making sure to remove paste residue from grooves and hidden areas.

* To clean a pewter piece, immerse it in water that has been used to boil eggs. Wait a few minutes, then gently rub the pewter with a soft cloth dipped in the same water. When the item is clean, rinse it with clear water and wipe dry.

* Ammonia is perfect for pewter polishing. Mix 2 tablespoons ammonia with 1 quart hot, soapy water. Wipe the surface of the pewter piece using a soft cotton cloth.

* To clean and shine copper or brass surfaces, combine equal parts salt and all-purpose flour and add enough distilled white vinegar to make a paste. Rub the paste on with a soft cloth. Let sit about 1 hour, then wipe off and buff with a clean, soft cloth.

* Use either of these pastes to clean brass or copper. For the first, mix lemon juice with either baking soda or cream of tartar to form a paste. The second combines lemon juice, salt, and corn meal. Rub the paste onto the brass or copper using a soft cloth; rinse and dry.

* Clean slightly tarnished brass or copper by rubbing with half a lemon or lime dipped in salt.

* Remove stubborn tarnish from copper by spraying stains with distilled white vinegar and sprinkling with salt. Scrub with a sponge, then rinse thoroughly, making sure to remove all traces of salt. Repeat if necessary.

* To remove "greenery" from brass and copper, rub the surface with a solution of equal parts ammonia and salt. Rinse with clear water.

* Remove marks on bronze by wiping bronze items with a soft cloth dampened ith turpentine.

MAKE IT YOURSELF!

GOLD CLEANER

Mix 1 teaspoon baking soda with enough water to form a paste. Rub the paste onto the gold object with a soft cloth, rinse, and buff dry with a chamois.

LACQUER

* To polish lacquered metal items, rub the surface with a soft cloth dampened with a few drops of extra virgin olive oil.

* The stronger, the better: Apply strongly brewed Lipton tea with a soft cloth to wash and polish black lacquer figurines and other decorative pieces. Use a second cloth to wipe dry.

VASES

❋ To clean a glass vase or similar container, fill it three-quarters full with hot water, add a teaspoon of baking soda, and shake. Let soak, then rinse.

❋ Remove mineral deposits or stains from a vase by dampening surfaces with water and sprinkling with salt. Wipe with a clean cloth.

❋ Clean stains from a vase by dropping 2 Alka-Seltzer tablets in the vase with water. Let sit, swish liquid around, and rinse.

❋ Get rid of stubborn spots on porcelain lamps, vases, and candlesticks by dipping a damp cloth in baking soda and rubbing them away. Wipe clean with a damp cloth.

CANDLES

❋ Wipe dirt from candles with a soft cloth, a folded paper towel, or a cotton ball dipped in isopropyl rubbing alcohol.

❋ You can forget about digging old, melted wax out of candlesticks. Before you insert a candle, coat the inside of the holder with petroleum jelly or baby oil.

❋ To release candle stubs and dripped wax that are stuck in or on candlesticks and holders, try soaking them in warm water or blasting them with a blow-dryer. A far neater and more effective method is putting the candlestick or holder in the freezer for at least 24 hours. The stub or wax drippings will slide away easily!

❋ Candle wax can be removed from most hard surfaces with a paste of baking soda and water. Scrub with a nylon scrubber.

MARBLE

Marble is used to make tabletops, floors, countertops, walls, steps, fireplace facings, window and door sills, other building materials, and statuary. It comes in a variety of colors and has either a shiny or a matte finish.

To clean marble, wipe with a damp, soft cloth that's been dipped into powdered chalk. Rinse with clear water, using another cloth or a sponge. Dry completely.

ALABASTER

Alabaster looks like marble and is made into vases, statues, lamp bases, and other ornamental objects. Although it comes in several colors and sometimes has a dark streak or band of color, the best-quality alabaster is pure white and translucent. It is fine-grained but soft enough to be scratched with a fingernail. Alabaster is easily broken, soiled, and weathered, and must be handled with care.

Dust alabaster frequently with a soft, untreated cloth or the small-brush attachment of your vacuum cleaner. We recommend that you gently blow dust away from intricate carving with the vacuum's blower.

An oil polish or soft wax will probably discolor alabaster, and abrasive or caustic cleaners will scratch it. Alabaster can be cleaned with commercial products that clean marble. **Caution:** Work in a well-ventilated area to avoid breathing fumes from these products; do not smoke while using them or work near an open flame because some marble-cleaning products are flammable.

MAKE IT YOURSELF!

ALABASTER CLEANER

Clean alabaster with borax; it is mild enough not to scratch the surface. Dip a moistened cloth into a small amount of dry borax and rub it on the alabaster. Rinse with warm water and buff dry with a soft cloth.

JADE

Jade is used to make lamp bases, vases, carved ornaments, and jewelry. It is hard, heavy, and fine-grained. The color of jade ranges from white to dark green, with occasional tints of brown, mauve, blue, yellow, red, gray, or black.

Because jade is hard and not porous, very little care is required. Dust it regularly, and buff it with a soft cloth or chamois when it begins to look dull. If a jade piece becomes soiled or sticky, wipe it with a damp cloth and buff it with a dry cloth.

ORGANIZATION & STORAGE

You can never find your keys. Or you put something away in a drawer, and when you need it again, you find it's gotten tangled or even broken. Here are some storage hacks to prevent those things from happening.

EVERYDAY ITEMS

* Hang a basket near the front door and keep your keys in it. You'll always know where they are. Also use this basket for bills and letters that need to be mailed. When you grab your keys, you'll remember to pick up the mail as well.

* Hang a wicker basket on the bathroom wall for storing towels, tissues, soap, or bath toys.

* Install two rows of coat hooks on your closet doors— one down low for a child to use, another higher up for you to use.

* A metal garbage can is perfect for storing long-handled yard tools. Hooks can also be attached to the outside of the can for hanging up smaller tools. You can lift up the whole can and move it to whichever part of the yard you're working in.

* Use an extra slot in the toothbrush holder to keep a medicine spoon handy.

* Keep toothbrushes handy but neatly out of the way on cup hooks attached to a wall or under a cabinet.

* Keep your wet umbrella in the shower where it can drip without making a mess. This is an especially useful strategy when you have company on a rainy day and everyone has an umbrella.

* A good place to store small clothing items is in large, metal potato-chip cans—after the cans are washed.

* Put a wine rack next to the door and use it to store your sandy beach shoes and muddy running or gardening shoes.

LIGHTS & BATTERIES

* Keep flashlight batteries fresh by storing them in a sealed plastic bag in the refrigerator.

* To minimize breakages, store loose light bulbs in tumblers. A paper towel wrapped around the bulb before you put it in the tumbler provides added protection.

LINENS

* Most people don't use good cloth tablecloths and napkins every night or even every week. To prevent the creases that form when linens are folded for storage, roll the linens onto cardboard tubes covered with cling wrap. Use paper towel tubes for napkins and gift wrap tubes for tablecloths.

* Incidentally, fine table linens are much easier to iron if you first place them in a plastic food storage bag and refrigerate them for 6 to 24 hours. Remove them from the bag before ironing!

* Keep place mats flat and out of the way by hanging them on a clipboard hung from a hook inside a cabinet or pantry door.

CORDS

To keep an appliance cord neat, store it in an old paper towel tube (use half a tube for short cords). Gather up the cord in loops a few inches longer than the tube; slide tube over looped cord. Label the tube with the name of the corresponding appliance.

BOOKS

Keep old books from becoming musty in storage. Before stowing them away, put a dryer sheet between the pages in a few places.

LUGGAGE

* Before storing a piece of luggage, place an open box of baking soda inside and close the luggage overnight. Repeat this when removing luggage from long-term storage.

* Send mildew odor packing: Toss a bar of scented bath soap into each piece of luggage before storing.

BREAKABLES

Breakables—from glass figurines to porcelain vases—need extra attention before you store them. Carefully place a breakable item in a plastic food storage bag that is just big enough to hold it. Seal the bag until it's almost closed. Blow up the bag with air, then run the seal the rest of the way. When you put the bag in a storage box or container, the item will be protected in a cushion of air.

BLANKETS

Freshen blankets that have been in storage by sprinkling with baking soda and rolling them up for a couple of hours. Shake out -baking soda, then fluff in the dryer without heat.

PAPER PRODUCTS

Smart shoppers take advantage of good deals. But where do you put all those rolls of toilet tissue and paper towels? Hang a pair of pantyhose on a nail or hook. Slide the rolls, one at a time, down each leg. Cut a hole at the bottom for dispensing; close it up with a twist tie or tie a loose knot until you need a roll.

CLEANING TOOLS

Cleaning tools with long handles or hoses—such as vacuum cleaner accessories, dryer vent cleaners, and ceiling fan dusters—are cumbersome to store. An old pair of pantyhose can "handle" the job. Hang a pair on a nail or hook, then slide the tools into the legs. If a tool has an extra-long handle, cut a very small hole in a toe of the pantyhose and insert it through the hole. The rest of the tool will stay in the leg.

NAILS & SCREWS

Glass baby-food jars are ideal for storing nails and screws. Better yet, nail the caps to a wood base or wall plaque, and just screw the jars into place.

CREATING MORE STORAGE SPACE

✳   If your home is built with studs and drywall, you can add cabinets between the studs, anywhere you need them—they won't take up any space at all. For example, put a liquor cabinet over your bar, or fashion a canned-goods pantry in your kitchen.

✳   Pegboard is most often used on walls, but it can also be used as a room divider or to make the inside of a closet or cabinet door more functional. When installing pegboard, remember to provide space behind the panels for the hooks.

✳   Use flat, roll-out bins for under-the-bed storage. They can hold bed linens, sewing supplies, and infrequently used items.

✳   To increase the capacity and efficiency of a drawer, outfit it with a lift-out tray. Fill the tray with items you frequently use, and use the space beneath the tray for articles you seldom need.

* Add more storage space in your bedroom by building a headboard storage unit. You can place books, lamps, or a radio on the lid of the unit and inside you can store extra linens and blankets.

* For extra closet storage, see if your closets can accommodate a second shelf above the existing one. If you install the main clothes-hanging rod high enough, you may be able to install another rod beneath it on which to hang shorter items such as slacks and shirts.

* A hallway can double as a storage area. Line it with shelves or shallow cabinets, or put shelving across the width of the hallway.

* If you're in need of an extra closet for storing items like golf clubs, skis, and camping equipment, angle a decorative folding screen across a little-used corner.

* Hooks, shelves, or hanging bins can transform the insides of closet doors into useful storage areas.

* Convert an ordinary closet or chest into a cedar closet or chest by installing thin cedar slats over inside surfaces. Then weather-strip to contain the scent.

* Use a stairway as a storage area by replacing ordinary nailed-in-place steps with hinged steps. The space under the hinged steps can hold boots or sports equipment.

* Put the space under a stairway to work as a storage area. Construct a wheeled, wedge-shaped container that fits into the area beneath the steps.

* To give yourself more storage space in a small bathroom, put up shelves on the dead wall space beside the vanity, over the toilet, or behind the door. Such shelves offer convenient storage without intruding on floor space.

* To make shelves without hammering a nail, upend two narrow wastebaskets on your closet shelf and position another shelf across them. Or use sturdy boxes stacked on their sides to make compartmented shelf space—you can see at a glance what's stored in the boxes, and you can use the tops for little-used items.

* If you have trouble with bubbles and creases when applying adhesive-backed paper to shelves or drawers, try smoothing the paper with a blackboard eraser.

SEPARATION ANXIETY

When you were a kid, you might have loved placing stickers on everything. As an adult, you worry more about what you'll do when they need to come off. No fear—we've got you covered.

* Remove adhesives, tape, glue, rubber cement, and labels from virtually all surfaces— even paint—with WD-40.
* Not only that, but with the help of WD-40, chewing gum can be removed from all manner of things, including hair, dryer lint screens, bed linens, linoleum floors, and aluminum siding.
* Use a bit of all-vegetable shortening to remove a label, price tag, or adhesive residue from glass, metal, and most kinds of plastic. Just cover the area with shortening. After 10 minutes, carefully scrub it clean with a no-scratch sponge.
* Remove an old sticker from a window, mirror, or other glass surface: Apply some mayonnaise to the area, wait a few minutes, and ease off the sticker with a flexible putty knife. Scrape gently if needed to remove stubborn adhesive.
* Safely scrape a decal, price tag, tape, or stuck-on paper from a wood surface by saturating the surface of the item to be removed with vegetable oil or dampening with vinegar. Let sit 10 minutes, then peel or gently scrape the sticker off. If it still won't budge, set your hair dryer on low and aim it at the item for half a minute. The heat will loosen the glue.

Painting a cabinet, a chair, or even a room is an easy way to freshen your home's design. These painting hacks will help.

PREPARING TO PAINT

✳ To avoid having to clean a paint tray, press a sheet of aluminum foil into it before use. When you're finished painting, simply wrap up the foil and dispose of it. You can also line the tray with a plastic bag, and then discard it when the job's done.

✳ Make a paint holder from a coat hanger to keep your hands free when painting. Open the hanger and bend it in half; then bend it into an "S" to hook over the ladder and hold your paint can.

✳ Before using a new paintbrush to apply oil-based paint, soak it for a day in a can of linseed oil. The brush will last longer and be easier to clean.

✳ Protect doorknobs when painting a door by wrapping the knobs with aluminum foil or by slipping plastic sandwich bags over them.

✳ Glue paper plates to the bottoms of paint cans to serve as drip catchers. The plates move along with the cans and are more convenient than newspapers.

✳ If you want to paint a window frame and have no masking tape, use strips of dampened newspaper. They will stick to the glass. Peel off the paper when you finish each frame.

* If your light-switch plate was painted over along with the wall and you now need to remove it, avoid flaking or chipping any paint by cutting carefully around the switch plate with a single-edge razor blade. Remove the screws and lift off the plate.

* If you don't want to—or can't—remove hardware when painting adjacent areas, coat the hardware with petroleum jelly before painting. You'll be able to wipe off any paint that accidentally gets on the metal.

WHEN TO PAINT

* When painting a ceiling with a roller, it's not necessary to try to keep the roller strokes all the same length. The lines won't show when the paint dries.

* If you're interrupted in the middle of a painting job, wrap aluminum foil or plastic wrap around your brushes and rollers. The wrapping should be loose enough to avoid mashing the bristles on brushes or the pile on rollers but tight enough to keep the air out. Leave the wrapped brushes on a flat surface or hang them up. Put the packet in the freezer to save the brush for a longer period of time.

* Prevent drips when painting a drawer front by removing the drawer and painting it face up.

* To avoid smearing while painting cabinets, paint the insides of the cabinets first. Then paint the tops, bottoms, and sides of doors before painting the door fronts. If you proceed in this sequence, you won't have to reach over already-painted areas.

* When painting stairs, paint alternate steps so that you'll have a way out. When those steps dry, paint the others. Or paint one side of each step at a time. Use the other side for foot traffic until the painted side dries, then reverse the process.

* Don't wipe your paintbrush against the lip of the paint can. The lip will soon fill up with paint that will run down the side and drip off. Use a coffee can to hold the paint instead.

* To cut the smell when you're decorating with oil-based paint, stir a spoonful of vanilla extract into each can of paint.

* If you want to be able to use a previous coat of exterior paint as a base for a new coat,

the old paint should be no more than five years old. If you wait longer than that you'll have a major job of scraping, sanding, and spackling.

* Wrinkling occurs when too much paint is applied or when the paint is too thick. You can correct wrinkling easily by sanding the surface and brushing on paint of a thinner consistency.

* Artificial light darkens color, so paint will look lighter in the daylight. If you're in doubt about a color at the paint store, take the container outside to examine the color.

* Color can saturate your eyes. When mixing paint, look away at a white surface for several minutes to allow your eyes to adjust so that you can judge the color accurately.

* To get the correct feel for spray painting and to determine the correct spray distance from the object to be painted, first experiment with a sheet of cardboard as the target area.

* Record how much paint is required to cover each room by writing the amount on the back of the light-switch plate. When you remove the switch plate before repainting, you'll be reminded of how much paint you need.

* To avoid painting a window shut, gently slide the sash up and down as the paint hardens but before it forms a seal.

* If you are working on a ladder in front of a closed door, lock the door so that no one can inadvertently swing the door open and send you sprawling.

* When tiny spots need a paint touch-up, use a cotton swab instead of a brush. You won't waste paint, and you won't have to clean a brush.

CLEANUP & STORAGE

* If the smell of fresh paint bothers you, you can eliminate it from a room in one day with a dish of ammonia, vinegar, or onion slices in water left out in the room.

* If you use masking tape around windows while painting the woodwork, remove the masking tape immediately after painting. Otherwise, it may pull off some of the paint.

* To get paint drips off hard-surface flooring, wrap a cloth around a putty knife and gently scrape up the paint. Then wash the areas with warm, soapy water. Don't use solvent; it can damage the finish on the floor.

* Why buy new paint thinner when you can reuse the old? Here's how: Pour paint thinner into an empty coffee can. After you've cleaned your brushes, cover the can tightly and let it stand for several days. When paint from the brushes has settled to the bottom as sediment, drain off the clean thinner into another can and store for reuse.

* To clean a paintbrush without making a mess of your hands, pour solvent into a strong, clear plastic bag, and insert the brush. Your hands will stay clean as you work the solvent into the bristles through the plastic.

* To clean a paint roller after use, roll it as dry as possible, first on the newly painted surface and then on several sheets of newspaper. Then slide the roller from its support and clean it with water or a solvent, depending on the type of paint used.

* Before capping leftover paint for storage, mark the label at the level of the remaining paint so you'll know without opening the can how much is left inside. Label the can with the room the paint was used for, so there's no question which paint to reorder or use for touch-ups.

* If you store a partially used can of paint upside down, skin won't form on the surface of the paint. (Be sure the lid is tight.)

* Leftover paint that is lumpy or contains shreds of paint skin can be strained through window screening.

* To keep a brush as soft as new, clean it and then rinse it in a solution of fabric softener and water.

* An empty coffee can with a plastic lid makes a perfect container for soaking brushes. Just make two slits in the center of the plastic lid to form an "X," push the brush handle up through the "X," and replace the lid. The lid seals the can so the solvent can't evaporate, and the brush is suspended without the bristles resting on the bottom.

* White paint won't yellow if you stir in a drop of black paint.

* You can remove paint spatters from your hair by rubbing the spots with baby oil.

* If you are cleaning brushes or rollers that have been used in oil-based paint, varnish, shellac, or lacquer, work in a well-ventilated area away from open flames.

* Before cleaning a brush, rid it of excess paint by tapping it against the inside rim of the can and then vigorously stroking the brush back and forth on a thick pad of folded newspapers until very little paint comes off.

* Clean brushes and rollers used for shellac in denatured alcohol, then wash in a detergent solution.

* Clean brushes or rollers used for lacquer in lacquer thinner or acetone and then wash in a detergent solution.

* Clean brushes or rollers used for oil-based paints and varnishes in turpentine or paint thinner and then wash in a detergent solution.

* Clean brushes and rollers used for latex paints in water and then wash in a detergent solution. Do not allow brushes to soak in water; this can loosen the bristles.

* Rinse all brushes well after washing and shake vigorously to remove excess water. Comb the bristles with a wire brush to straighten them. Then allow the brush to dry completely before storing it flat or hanging from a rack.

DESIGN & DECORATION

Your pictures, prints, and decorations help turn your house into a home. These design and decoration strategies will help.

PICTURES

* If a picture won't hang straight, wrap masking tape around the wire on both sides of the hook so that the wire can't slip. Or install parallel nails or hooks a short distance apart; two hooks are better than one for keeping pictures in their places.

* Squares of double-faced tape affixed to the two lower-back corners of the frame will keep a picture from moving. If you don't have double-faced tape, make two loops with masking tape, sticky side out. Apply to each of the lower-back corners and press the picture against the wall.

* Take the guesswork out of arranging several pictures on a wall. Spread a large sheet of wrapping paper or several taped-together sheets of newspaper on the floor and experiment with frame positions. When you decide on a pleasing grouping, outline the frames on the paper, tape the paper to the wall, and drive hooks through the paper into the wall. Then remove the paper and hang the pictures.

* Picture hanging can be frustrating if you simply try to eyeball the right spot to put the hook. Instead, place a picture exactly where you want it the first time with the following method: Cut a sheet of paper to the exact size of the frame. Position the pattern on the back of the picture, pull up taut the wire the picture will hang from, and mark the inverted "V" point on the pattern. Adjust the pattern on the wall, and then poke through it to mark the "V" point on the wall. If you nail the hook there, the picture will hang precisely where you wanted it.

* If the picture isn't too heavy, another timesaving method is to hold the picture itself by its wire and decide where you want it positioned. Wet a fingertip and press it on the wall to mark the wire's inverted "V" point. The fingerprint mark will stay wet long enough for you to drive a nail or hook on target.

* Don't lose a perfect picture grouping when you repaint a room—insert toothpicks in the hook holes and paint right over them; when the paint dries, remove the toothpicks and rehang your pictures.

* To prevent a plaster wall from crumbling when driving in a nail or hook, first form an "X" over the nail spot with two strips of masking tape or transparent tape.

* If you're hanging a picture from a molding but don't like the look of exposed picture wire, substitute nylon fishing line. The transparent nylon does a disappearing act that allows your picture to star on its own.

* Hang heavy objects by driving nails directly into the wood studs behind walls. There are several ways to locate studs. You can tap a wall gently with your knuckles or a hammer. A wall sounds hollow between studs, solid on top of them. Or move an electric razor (turned on) along a wall; a razor registers a different tone over studs. If nails were used to attach drywall to studs, a magnet will indicate the location of the nails and, therefore, the studs.

* Sometimes a picture that has been hanging for a while will leave a dark outline on the wall because dust and dirt have collected against the frame. To prevent this buildup, allow better air circulation by holding pictures slightly away from the wall with thumb tacks pressed firmly into the backs of their frames. You can get the same result by fixing small tabs of self-sticking foam weather stripping to the picture backing.

MIRRORS

* When hanging a mirror with screws that go through mounting holes in the glass, don't tighten the screws all the way. Leave enough play to prevent the mirror from cracking if the wall shifts.

* Hang mirrors to reflect you but not the sun; some mirror backings are adversely affected by direct sunlight.

DESIGN

＊ A room will appear larger if you paint an oversized piece of furniture the same color as the walls.

＊ A small room can be made to look larger if you install mirrors on one wall to reflect the rest of the room.

＊ The texture of your furnishings can brighten or darken a room. Glossy surfaces like satin, glass, and tile reflect light and add brightness to a room; surfaces like brick, carpet, and burlap absorb light and make a room seem less bright.

＊ In a room with a low ceiling, use vertical lines—high-backed chairs, straight draperies—to carry the eye upward and give an illusion of height. Horizontal lines—a long sofa or low bookcases—give a feeling of space and make high ceilings appear lower.

＊ Small rooms will seem even smaller if filled with elaborate patterns or designs. Keep the furniture for a small room simple and the colors fairly restrained.

＊ A darker color on the ceiling will make a room with a high ceiling seem more in proportion. So will low-placed, eye-catching objects such as a low coffee table, low-slung chairs, and plants on the floor.

＊ In a long, narrow room, paint the end walls contrasting colors for a striking effect. Room dividers or furniture positioned in the middle of the room will give the effect of two rooms in one and lessen the feeling of length.

＊ A favorite painting can be the inspiration for the color scheme of a room. Select one dominant color and several contrasting shades to create a pleasing combination.

＊ If you use the same fabric on two different chairs, it will tie the decor of the room together.

＊ To add color to matchstick blinds, weave rows of colored ribbon through them.

＊ Matchstick blinds can disguise a wall of hobby or utility shelves for a clean, unified look. They also can be used to partition off a closet or dressing area.

＊ There is no need to invest in drapes if your budget is tight. Instead, brighten up inexpensive shades by decorating them with tape to complement the wall color or wallpaper, or by gluing fabric over them.

* To give a room a soft glow, spotlight objects in a room instead of lighting the whole room. For example, light a piece of art or a bookcase.

* Hang shiny, metallic blinds vertically or horizontally to help reflect summer sun. This works especially well in south and west windows.

* You can make a curtain panel from a bed sheet by knotting the top corners around a bamboo pole.

* A screen of hanging plants can be a great substitute for curtains.

* For an insulating window covering, attach wood rings to a patchwork quilt and hang it from a wood rod. Don't do this, however, if the quilt is an antique that could fade or otherwise be damaged by exposure to sunlight.

* Turn your bathroom into a miniature gallery with pictures that can't be damaged by humidity.

* Keep your decorative baskets looking healthy by placing them away from dry heat and rinsing them periodically with clear water to remove dust and restore moisture.

* Display flowers in unusual vases—a crystal ice bucket, a fluted champagne glass, a bright coffee mug, or a jug. Flowers, in fact, look good in almost any container.

* For a quick, easy, and inexpensive way to re-cover a chair, drape a twin-size sheet over the chair, and tie or pin the corners to fit. You can use the same trick to add interest to a small table.

* An easy way to give a room a new look is to update hardware, such as doorknobs, drawer pulls, and curtain rods.

* Replace the drab cord or chain on a light fixture with a piece of satin piping or silver cord. Thread a bright ceramic bead at the end of the cord for a finishing touch.

* Glue pieces of felt to the rough bottoms of vases and art objects to keep them from scratching tables.

∗ Use leftover dining room wallpaper to make matching place mats. Paste the paper onto sturdy cardboard, trim the edges neatly, and coat each mat with a plastic spray.

∗ An old dining table found at a flea market can become a sofa-height coffee table. Just cut the legs to the height you need.

∗ You can make unusual centerpieces in no time by floating flowers in clear glass dishes. Fill the dishes halfway with water, cut the stems from the flowers, and place them in the dishes.

∗ Old, carved doorknobs, attached to each end of a dowel, make an attractive curtain rod. Paint or stain the knobs to match your furniture.

∗ You can make cheap floor rugs by stenciling canvas with nontoxic acrylic paints.

∗ Make an extra closet into a book nook for quiet reading. Remove the door, and install a wall lamp, shelves, and a comfortable chair.

∗ You can make inexpensive bookcases out of flue tiles or conduit pipes. The cubbyholes are perfect for storing wine.

YOUR HOME SHOP

If you own your own home, you likely have a corner of the garage and basement filled with tools of all sorts. It can be a jumbled mess, or it can be a tidy resource. Here's how to make it more the latter than the former.

* To protect tools, store them where they aren't subjected to moisture. Keep a thin coating of oil on metal parts, wrap them in plastic wrap, or keep carpenter's chalk, which absorbs moisture, in the toolbox.

* To sharpen scissors, snip pieces of sandpaper.

* A piece of garden hose, slit open, is a handy protective cover for the teeth of a handsaw between projects.

* Clean tools without expensive cleaners:
Pour a small amount of kerosene onto the metal parts of a tool and rub vigorously with a soap-filled steel-wool pad. Then wad a piece of aluminum foil into a ball and rub on the surface. Wipe away the residue with newspaper, and coat the tool lightly with olive oil before storing. **Caution:** Kerosene is flammable; do not use it near an open flame.

* If you hang tools on pegboard walls, outline the tools with paint so you'll know at a glance where each tool goes. You'll also know when a tool hasn't been replaced.

* If you want to remind yourself to unplug an electric drill when changing accessories, fasten the chuck key near the plug end of the cord.

* Paint all tool handles with an unusual bright color, or wrap reflective tape around them; they'll be easy to identify if borrowed or left in the wrong place.

* Don't take a chance of hitting a thumb or finger when hammering a small brad, tack, or nail. Slip the fastener between the teeth of a pocket comb; the comb holds the nail while you hold the comb. A bobby pin or a paper clip can be used the same way as a comb.

* Here's a homemade rust-preventive coating for tools, outdoor furniture, and other metal objects: Combine ¼ cup lanolin and 1 cup petroleum jelly in a double boiler over low heat. Stir until the mixture melts and blends completely, then remove from heat and pour into a clean jar, letting the mixture cool partially. Use the mixture while it's still warm. Don't wipe it off—just let it dry on the object. If you have leftover coating, cover it tightly, and rewarm it before you use it again.

* An empty soft-drink carton makes a convenient kit for holding and carrying lubricants.

* To keep the pores of your hands dirt- or grease-free, wipe on a thin coat of petroleum jelly before starting a messy task.

* You won't waste time when picking up spilled nails, screws, or tacks if you collect them with a magnet covered with a paper towel. When the spilled items snap toward the magnet, gather the towel corners over the pieces and then pull the towel bag away from the magnet.

* As an aid in measuring lumber or pipe, paint lines a foot apart on your shop or garage floor.

* You can prevent a knot in nylon rope from working loose by holding it briefly over a small flame. The heat will melt and bond the fibers.

* Know the exact width of your hand so you can make rough measurements without using a ruler or tape measure.

* Loosen a stubborn screw, bolt, or nut with a shot of penetrating oil. If you don't have oil, use hydrogen peroxide, white vinegar, kerosene, or household ammonia. Should these prove ineffective, heat the metal with an iron, rap it sharply with a hammer while it's still hot, and try again to loosen it. **Caution:** Kerosene is flammable; do not use it near an open flame.

* You can often loosen rusted bolts by pouring a carbonated beverage on them.

* If a bolt repeatedly loosens due to vibrations, coat the threads with fingernail polish and reinsert it. When you need to remove it, you can break the seal with a little effort.

* If you don't have a carpenter's level, you can substitute a straight-sided jar with a lid. Fill the jar three-quarters full of water. Lay it on its side on the surface you're testing – when the water is level, the surface is, too.

* For easy workshop measuring, fasten a yardstick to the edge of your workbench. Cut keyhole slots in the yardstick so you can remove it when you need it elsewhere.

* If you're out of penetrating oil, you can substitute hydrogen peroxide or lemon juice.

* An old nylon stocking makes an effective strainer if you're out of cheesecloth.

* You can use a coping saw blade to remove a broken-off key from a lock. Slide the blade in beside the key, turn it toward the key so its teeth sink into the key's soft brass, and then pull the blade out along with the key fragment.

* To prevent metal tubing from denting when sawing it, insert a dowel that fits the tube's interior tightly.

* Dipping the ends of a rope in shellac, varnish, or paint will keep them from unraveling.

* To hide a screw head, drill a counter-bored hole, seat the screw, glue a dowel into the counter-bore and sand it flush.

SLEEP TIGHT

Bedspreads, blankets, mattresses, quilts—all require care and attention. These tips will help you keep them in good shape for a long time.

BEDSPREADS

Many bedspreads are washable. Before you wash your bedspread, dip a corner of it in the detergent solution you plan to use to check for colorfastness. If the color bleeds, have your bedspread dry cleaned.

* If it is safe to wash your bedspread, we advise you to wash it before it becomes heavily soiled. Treat spots and stains with a spray prewash product or liquid detergent.
* Use a large commercial washing machine for oversized bedspreads. An overcrowded washer won't clean very well.
* Dry bedspreads across several clotheslines or in a large commercial dryer.

BLANKETS

Blankets are made of many different fibers and blends, but most of them are washable by hand or machine. Some wool blankets can be machine washed, some cannot. Check the care label and follow the manufacturer's instructions.

* Air blankets on a clothesline periodically to refresh them.
* Before you wash a blanket, mend or replace bindings and treat spots and stains. Use a large commercial washer to wash large blankets. Fill the washer with water and put in the detergent so it can completely dissolve before you add the blanket. Use a gentle (delicate) wash cycle; long periods of agitation will mat blanket fibers.

Also avoid overcrowding the machine. A fabric softener will increase a blanket's fluffiness and reduce static electricity.

* When washing cotton or washable wool blankets, add 2 cups vinegar to the rinse cycle. This will help remove soap and make blankets soft and fluffy.

DOWN-FILLED COMFORTERS & QUILTS

The down filling in some comforters and quilts is held in place by tufts of yarn or by stitched-through patterns. Most down-filled comforters and quilts are washable, but some older ones are too fragile to be cleaned at home.

* Follow the manufacturer's care instructions if they are available. Test older comforters and quilts for colorfastness by wetting an inconspicuous spot with the detergent solution you plan to use and blotting the area with a white blotter.
* If comforters or quilts are in good condition, machine wash and dry them. Use cold wash water and rinse water and all-purpose detergent. Fragile down comforters and quilts should be hand washed in the bathtub or a deep laundry tub.
* Drape the wet comforter or quilt over several clotheslines to allow excess moisture to drip out; reposition it periodically. If the comforter or quilt is strong enough to be dried in a clothes dryer, preheat the dryer to a low temperature and include a pair of clean, dry sneakers to help fluff the down. The dryer can also be set on air dry (no heat) to dry the quilt.

WOOL-, COTTON-, & SYNTHETIC-FILLED COMFORTERS & QUILTS

* Most cotton- or polyester-filled comforters and quilts are washable, but older quilts may be too delicate to withstand washing.

* Some newer wool-filled or wool-covered comforters and quilts can be washed at home; others should be dry-cleaned.

* Follow the manufacturer's care instructions if they are available. Test old quilts and comforters for colorfastness before attempting to wash them by wetting a small area with the detergent solution and blotting it with a white blotter.

* Clean patchwork quilts with the method that is appropriate for the most delicate fabric in the quilt. Never attempt to wash silk- or velvet-covered quilts and comforters.

* For small- to medium-size quilts and comforters, use your home washing machine. For large quilts, use a commercial washer. Let quilts and comforters soak in the machine for about 10 minutes before starting them through a short, gentle (delicate) washing cycle.

* Hand wash and line-dry old or fragile quilts and all quilts with cotton batting. Machine washing is too harsh and can cause cotton batting to bunch up. Use a bathtub or deep laundry tub, and allow the soap or detergent to dissolve in the wash water before adding the quilt.

MATTRESS & BOX SPRINGS

* Vacuum mattresses and box springs, and turn the mattress over and around end-to-end to ensure even wear. Use an upholstery attachment on your vacuum cleaner, and work carefully around any buttons on your mattress. Remove dust and blanket fluff from the edges of the box spring with your vacuum brush attachment.

* Cover mattresses with quilted or rubberized pads that can be quickly washed when they become soiled.

* Remove spots and stains promptly, but do not allow the mattress to become excessively wet when you spot clean it.

* Do not make the bed until the mattress is completely dry.

PILLOWS

✳ Protect your pillows with a zip-on cotton or polyester cover, which you can wash regularly. Refresh pillows by airing them near an open window or hanging them on a clothesline outside.

✳ Kapok is the silky covering of seeds from the ceiba tree; pillows with this stuffing need frequent airing but cannot be washed.

✳ Fluff down and feather pillows when you make your bed to get rid of accumulated dust and to redistribute the filling. Before you wash a feather or down pillow, make sure it has no holes or ripped seams. Machine or hand wash feather and down pillows in cool water with cold-water, light-duty detergent. Wash two pillows at a time or add a couple of bath towels to balance the load. If the fabric is worn or the pillow is heavily stuffed, wash the feathers and ticking separately. Secure the feathers in a large muslin bag and stitch the opening closed.

✳ Dry down and feather pillows in the dryer on the low-heat setting. Including a pair of clean, dry tennis shoes in the dryer will help distribute the down as it dries.

✳ Hand wash and line-dry foam pillows. Change the hanging position hourly to dry the filling evenly. Never put a foam pillow in the dryer.

✳ For polyester-filled pillows, read the care-instruction tags; some polyester-filled pillows are washable, but some are not. Machine or hand wash polyester-filled pillows in warm water with an all-purpose detergent. A front-loading tumble washer rather than a top-loading machine works best for polyester pillows. Dry the pillows in the dryer on a moderate heat setting.

LAUNDRY

When we think about laundry, we often imagine snow-white sheets billowing in the breeze, shirts with no telltale stains or rings around the collars, glimmering little-league uniforms, and baby-soft, sweet-smelling piles of neatly folded clothes. The reality of laundry is less exciting. But if you don't keep up with the laundry, you won't have anything to wear. Since you have to do it, make it as easy as you can. We're here to help speed you through piles of laundry, with guidelines and tips on how to care for everything from your favorite sweatshirt to your best shirt.

YOUR LAUNDRY ROOM/THE LAUNDROMAT

* Opening a detergent box with a pour spout can be hazardous to your fingernails. Use a "church key" bottle opener—the flat end will probably work best.

* Freshen laundry hampers by sprinkling baking soda over dirty clothes as they await washing.

* To mask the odor of dirty laundry, keep a dryer sheet in the bottom of your laundry basket, bag, or hamper.

* Make an impromptu garment bag: Cut a hole in the center of the bottom seam of a trash bag (unscented, twist-tie variety). Turn it upside down and place over a hanger.

* Don't lug all those boxes and bottles to the Laundromat. Instead, put a load of laundry into a pillowcase, then pour in the right amount of powdered detergent and bleach for the load. Just dump it all into the washer!

✳   Save energy (your own!) en route to the Laundromat by premeasuring detergents or other products into plastic tubs or plastic bags.

UNDERSTANDING FABRIC CARE LABELS

The first step toward doing your laundry quickly and efficiently is to know what an item is made of and the best way to care for it. Most garments and many other fabric items manufactured and sold in the United States have permanently attached care labels. These labels are also required on garments made of suede and leather. They can be of enormous help in determining exactly how you should remove stains and clean an item.

Certain information is not included on care labels. Neither the manufacturer nor the retailer is required to inform a consumer that a certain fabric will shrink.

The label assumes that the purchaser knows that an item labeled "hand wash" should be washed in lukewarm water and that all nonwhite articles should not be treated with chlorine bleach.

Another important piece of information contained on fabric care labels is the fiber content of the material. This is especially important with blends. These fabrics are combinations of fibers, such as cotton and wool, cotton and polyester, or wool and acrylic. Blends should be cared for in the same way as the fiber with the *highest percentage in the blend.* For example, a blend of 60 percent cotton and 40 percent polyester should be cleaned as though it were 100 percent cotton. However, when you remove spots and stains, you should follow procedures recommended for the *most delicate fiber in the blend.* For example, to remove stains from a blend of cotton and silk, use the procedure recommended for silk. If after such treatment the stain is still apparent, follow the procedure for cotton, the most durable fiber in this blend.

COTTON

Cotton fabric is strong, long-wearing, and absorbent. It will shrink and wrinkle unless it is given special treatment. Cotton is often blended with other fibers or treated with a finish to make it wrinkle-resistant. It is available in a wide variety of weights and textures, from denim or corduroy to percale.

* Machine wash and tumble-dry cotton fabrics, using a water temperature ranging from cold to hot, depending on the manufacturer's care instructions, and an all-purpose detergent.
* If needed, a chlorine bleach can be used on white or colorfast cotton unless a fabric finish has been applied. Do not use more than the recommended amount of bleach; this can damage the fibers.
* We recommend that you use fabric softener to improve softness and to reduce wrinkling. But fabric softener makes cotton less absorbent and should not be used on towels, washcloths, or diapers.
* Pretreat oil-based spots and stains with a prewash.
* Wash and shrink cotton fabrics before using them for home sewing.
* Iron cotton with a hot iron for best results and use spray starch or spray sizing to restore its crisp appearance.

LINEN

Pure linen fabric wrinkles easily, so many manufacturers make linen blends or add wrinkle-resistant finishes to overcome this problem. Linen is absorbent and comfortable to wear, but it can crack or show wear at the seams, along the creases, and at the finished edges of the garment.

* Machine wash and tumble-dry linen. An all-purpose detergent is the best cleaning agent, and chlorine bleach can be used on white linen, following the manufacturer's recommended amount so as not to damage the fabric.
* Linen can also be dry-cleaned. It should be pressed with a hot iron while it is still slightly damp for the best results.

SILK

Silk is a delight to wear, but it requires special care. Most silk garments are marked "dry-clean only." However, some silk can be washed by hand. A piece of silk fabric that you are going to make into a garment should first be washed by hand.

* We suggest that you always test a corner of the fabric for colorfastness before washing a whole piece of silk. Some dyed silk will bleed.
* Use a hair shampoo containing protein and warm or cool water for hand washing; the protein in the shampoo feeds the protein in the silk.
* Handle washable silk gently during washing; never twist or wring it.
* Hang silk out of direct sunlight to drip-dry.
* Press silk while it is still damp with a warm iron (below 275 degrees Fahrenheit) or use a steam iron.
* To remove stains from washable white or light-colored silk, use only oxygen bleach or mix 1 part hydrogen peroxide (3 percent) to 8 parts water.

WOOL

Wool fabric is highly resilient, absorbent, and sheds wrinkles well, but wool will shrink and mat if it's exposed to heat and rubbing. Popular in both knit and woven fabrics, the textures of wool fabrics range from fine wool crepe and jersey to felt and mohair.

* Treat spots and stains on wool fabrics with solvent-based spot removers. Clean felt by wiping it with a dry sponge. For a more thorough treatment, hold the material over steam from a teakettle, and brush lightly with a dry sponge or lint-free cloth to smooth the surface.
* Wool should always be dry-cleaned unless it is specifically marked "washable."
* Use light-duty detergent in cold water to wash wool. Allow the article to soak for a few minutes before starting the washing process. Handle woolens carefully when they are wet to avoid stretching. Machine washing is appropriate only if the care label indicates that it is, and then use only cold water and the gentle cycle.
* Remove excess moisture by rolling a wool article in a towel, then block it into shape and dry it on a flat surface. Only machine-dry woolens if the manufacturer's instructions recommend it.
* Press wool with a hot iron, using lots of steam. Cover the article with a damp cloth or chemically treated press cloth. Allow the garment to dry thoroughly before storing it.

ACETATE

Acetate is made from cellulose and has a silk-like appearance. Closely related to rayon, it has good body and drapes well. Taffeta, satin, crepe, brocade, and double knits often contain acetate. It is not very absorbent or colorfast, and acetate loses its strength when it is wet.

* Hand wash acetate carefully in warm water, using a light-duty detergent, if the care label specifies that the article is washable; otherwise have it dry-cleaned. Do not soak colored items or wash them with white articles. Add fabric softener to the rinse water to reduce wrinkles.
* Line-dry acetate away from heat or direct sunlight. Press at the coolest setting, on the wrong side, while the article is damp. Use a press cloth when pressing the right side of the fabric.
* Nail-polish remover and perfumes will permanently damage acetate.

ACRYLIC

Many acrylic weaves resemble wool's softness, bulk, and fluffiness. Acrylics are wrinkle-resistant and usually are machine washable. Often acrylic fibers are blended with wool or polyester fibers. Acrylic's biggest drawback is its tendency to pill. Blends will do this less than pure acrylic.

* Dry-clean acrylic garments or wash them by hand or in the machine.
* Pretreat oil-based stains, and turn garments inside out before laundering to reduce pilling.
* Wash delicate items by hand in warm water, gently squeezing out the water.
* Machine wash sturdy articles with an all-purpose detergent, and tumble-dry at low temperatures.
* If the fabric is labeled "colorfast," it can be bleached with either chlorine or oxygen bleach. We've found that adding fabric softener to the rinse water every third or fourth time an article is washed reduces static electricity.
* Press at a moderate temperature setting, using steam.

NYLON

Nylon fabrics are extremely strong, lightweight, smooth, and lustrous. They are also nonabsorbent and have excellent abrasion- and wrinkle-resistance. Often combined with spandex, nylon knits are very stretchy but hold and recover their original shape. Available in many textures, nylon is used to make all kinds of items, including lingerie, carpets, rainwear, and tents.

✳   Always follow the manufacturer's cleaning instructions.
✳   Pretreat oil-based stains on nylon.
✳   Machine wash sturdy articles in warm water with an all-purpose detergent.
✳   Hand wash lingerie and hosiery, using warm water and light-duty detergent, or machine wash in a mesh bag to prevent stretching or tearing. Do not launder white nylon with colored fabrics of any kind.
✳   Use a chlorine bleach only if a nylon article is colorfast, and use fabric softener to reduce static electricity.
✳   Tumble-dry nylon at a low temperature setting.
✳   Press at a cool temperature setting.

POLYESTER

Polyester fabrics are strong, resilient, wrinkle-resistant, colorfast, and crisp. They hold pleats and creases well, but they are also nonabsorbent, attract and hold oil-based stains, may pill when rubbed, and may yellow with age. Polyester is used for clothing and filling; some bed linens and towels are also made from polyester blends.

✳   Polyester can be safely dry-cleaned or machine washed.
✳   Pretreat oil-based stains with prewash or all-purpose liquid detergent.
✳   Turn polyester-knit garments inside out before washing to prevent snags.
✳   Machine wash polyester in warm water using an all-purpose detergent, and tumble-dry at a low temperature setting. Use a chlorine bleach if necessary. Using a fabric softener will reduce static electricity.
✳   Do not overdry polyester; this will cause gradual shrinkage. Press polyester fabrics at a moderate temperature setting or use steam.

RAYON

Rayon is a strong, absorbent fabric, but it tends to lose its strength when it is wet. It is used for drapery and upholstery fabrics as well as for clothing.

* Dry-clean rayon or wash it by hand unless it is labeled "machine washable."
* For hand wash, use lukewarm water with a light-duty detergent. Squeeze moisture out gently when washing rayon fabrics by hand.
* Machine wash rayon in warm water on a gentle cycle with a light-duty detergent.
* Chlorine bleach can be used on rayon unless it has been treated with a resin finish.
* Drip-dry and press rayon on the wrong side with an iron at a medium temperature setting while the fabric is damp.

SPANDEX

Spandex is a lightweight fiber that resembles rubber in durability. It has good stretch and recovery, and it is resistant to damage from sunlight, abrasion, and oils. Always blended with other fibers, spandex provides the stretch in waistbands, foundation garments, swimwear, and dancewear.

* Pretreat oil-based stains.
* Hand or machine wash spandex-blend garments in warm water using an all-purpose detergent.
* Do not wash white spandex with colored fabrics of any kind. Use only oxygen or sodium-perborate bleach. Rinse thoroughly.
* Line-dry or tumble-dry garments made with spandex at a low temperature setting.
* Press clothing that contains spandex rapidly, if needed, using a low temperature setting.

TRIACETATE

Triacetate resembles acetate, but it is less sensitive to heat. This allows triacetate to be creased and crisply pleated. Triacetate is often a component in jersey, textured knits, and taffeta.

* Pleated garments can be hand or machine washed in cold water.
* Set the gentle cycle to agitate for 3 minutes. Drip-dry permanently pleated garments, or air-dry them in dryer.
* Most triacetate articles can be machine washed with an all-purpose detergent in hot or warm water. Tumble- or line-dry triacetate. Press, if necessary, using a hot temperature setting.

LAUNDRY TECHNIQUES

You could jam all your dirty laundry in the washing machine, run it through whatever wash cycle happens to be programmed, and hope for the best. This method may leave your sweater doll-sized or turn your white silk shirt pink, but it's quick—if you don't count the time you'll spend replacing your ruined clothes. Doing your laundry properly will take more time. Your clothes will last longer and look better if you pay careful attention to sorting, pretreating, water temperature, machine cycle, and the right laundry products for each particular fabric.

Properly sorting the laundry is the first step to a clean wash and helps to keep your clothes, linens, and other household items looking their best through repeated washings.

Color: First sort the laundry by color. Put all the white or predominantly white articles in one pile, the light colors and pastels in another pile, and the bright and dark-colored items into a third. Then separate the dark pile into two piles: one for colorfast items and one for noncolorfast items.

Degree of soil: Separate each pile into three smaller piles: lightly soiled, moderately soiled, and heavily soiled.

Compatible loads: Now you have up to 12 various-sized piles of laundry. Combine or divide the piles to come up with compatible, washer-sized loads. The following hints will help you with your final sorting:

* Combine white and light-colored items that have similar degrees of soil into the same pile.

- ✳ Combine noncolorfast items with similarly colored colorfast items with the same degree of soil.
- ✳ Create a separate pile for delicate items that must be hand washed.
- ✳ Separate white synthetic articles, and wash them only with other white fabrics.
- ✳ Separate synthetics, blends, and permanent-press fabrics from natural-fiber fabrics without special finishes.
- ✳ Separate items made from fabrics that produce lint, such as chenille robes and bath towels, from fabrics that attract lint, such as corduroy, knits, synthetics, and permanent press.

PREPARING THE WASH

Know the fiber content and finishes of fabrics so you can select the proper water temperature and cleaning products.

- ✳ Save care information so you can follow the recommended cleaning procedures.
- ✳ Close all zippers, hook all hooks, and button all buttons.
- ✳ Turn pockets inside out to get rid of debris.
- ✳ Remove nonwashable trim or decorations and pins or buckles that might make holes or snag other articles in the wash.
- ✳ Tie or buckle all belts and sashes to prevent tangling.
- ✳ Mend seams, tears, holes, or loose hems to prevent further damage during the wash cycle.
- ✳ Turn sweaters and corduroy garments inside out to prevent pilling and to combat their tendency to collect lint.
- ✳ Pretreat spots, stains, and heavily soiled items with prewash spot-and-stain remover, liquid detergent, a paste made from granular soap or detergent, a bar of soap, or a presoak solution.
- ✳ Remove the smell of cigarette smoke from clothes by soaking them in a solution of 4 tablespoons baking soda and 1 quart water before washing.
- ✳ Use equal parts water and vinegar to pretreat common stains on clothing. Spray mixture on stains before washing to give an extra boost.

* Pretreat collar stains on shirts with cornstarch. Dampen collar, rub a little in, and launder as usual.

PREWASH SPOT-AND-STAIN REMOVERS

While soaps and detergents can be worked directly into spots and heavily soiled areas before you put the laundry into the washer, a special product designed just for removing spots and stains is more convenient to use. Called prewash spot-and-stain removers, these aerosols or pump sprays are excellent for spot treating stubborn soil, especially grease marks on synthetic fabrics.

Treat the stain while it is still fresh. Saturate the soiled area completely, then lightly rub the fabric together to work the prewash product into the fibers.

Some prewash products can damage the exterior finish of your washer and dryer, so be careful where you spray them.

PRESOAKS

Granular presoak products containing enzymes break down some stubborn stains such as milk, blood, baby formula, chocolate, gravy, fruits and vegetables, and grass. Presoaks are not effective on rust, ink, oil, or grease.

* Following the manufacturer's directions, mix a solution in a large sink or in the washer. Before adding the soiled laundry, make sure that the presoak has dissolved thoroughly.
* Soak clothes for the recommended length of time; an overnight soak is suitable for articles that look dull and dingy.
* Do not soak dark- and light-colored fabrics together for long periods of time; this can cause colors to run.
* Wash the laundry as usual after using a presoak.
* You can use presoaks for diaper-pail solutions and as detergent boosters.

LAUNDRY PRODUCTS

Most commercial laundry preparations are designed to be used in washing machines, but some can be used for both hand and machine washing. Read the label carefully before purchasing any product to make sure it is the right one for the job you want it to do. When you use a laundry product, follow the directions precisely and measure accurately.

Water Conditioners: The amount and type of chemicals and minerals dissolved in water determines whether it is hard or soft. The condition of the water affects the cleaning potential of laundry products: The softer the water, the more effective it is for cleaning. Determine the hardness of your water so you will know if you need to condition it for effective cleaning.

Hard water leaves a residue on articles you launder; this is known as washing film. To soften water, the minerals must be removed or chemically locked up. Water that measures under four grains hardness per gallon will probably clean effectively, especially if a detergent rather than soap is used. You can soften hard water with a mechanical water softener that attaches to your home's water tank or by adding a water-conditioning product to the wash and rinse water.

Follow the directions on product labels precisely.

Wash flame-retardant items only in soft water.

Use a water conditioner to remove previously formed washing film or soap/detergent buildup. You can also remove hard-water washing film from diapers, towels, or fabrics by soaking them in a solution of 1 cup white vinegar and 1 gallon water in a plastic container.

Use a water softener if you use soap in hard water or if you use a phosphate-free detergent.

Detergents and Soaps: Soap is a mixture of alkalis and fats that is a good cleaner in soft water, breaks down well in city sewer systems, and does not harm the environment. Soap is less

155

effective in hard water, however, because it reacts with the high mineral content to form soap curd, which leaves a gray scum on clothing.

Detergents are synthetic washing products derived from petroleum and other nonfatty materials. They are less affected by hard water than soap and have excellent cleaning power. Since detergents contain a wetting agent that lifts off dirt and agents that help to make hard water minerals inactive, they do not create scum.

It was once common for detergents to contain phosphates, which are harmful to the environment because they promote an overgrowth of algae in water, but store-bought detergents today are phosphate-free. The cleaning ability of phosphate-free detergents is less effective in hard water and in cold-water washes than detergents that contain phosphates, and these detergents may cause excessive wear to some fabrics.

Always follow the manufacturer's instructions for the amount of detergent to use, the proper wash cycle, and the recommended water temperature. Measure carefully, but use extra detergent for heavy and/or greasy soil, larger-than-normal loads, and warm- or cold-water washes.

You may also need more than the manufacturer's recommended amount of detergent if you have hard water and when you use phosphate-free detergent. Adding 1 cup ammonia to the wash water will boost detergent effectiveness for heavily soiled or greasy wash loads.

Use liquid detergents in cold-water washes for best results, or dissolve powder or granular detergents in 1 quart hot water, then add the solution to the cold wash water.

Bleach: Bleach works with detergent or soap to remove stains and soil, whiten white items, and brighten the colors of some fabrics. It also acts as a mild disinfectant. The two basic types of laundry bleach are chlorine and oxygen. Common liquid chlorine bleach is the most effective and least expensive, but it cannot be used on all fabrics. Oxygen bleach is safer for all washable fabrics, resin-finished fibers, and most washable colors, but it is much less strong than chlorine bleach.

Always give colored fabrics a colorfastness test before using any bleach by mixing 1 tablespoon chlorine bleach with ¼ cup warm water or; 1 tablespoon oxygen bleach with 2 quarts hot water.

Apply the solution to an inconspicuous place; wait a few minutes and check for a color change. If the color does not bleed, use the bleach according to the manufacturer's directions.

Add diluted chlorine bleach to the wash water about five minutes after the wash cycle has begun or use the automatic bleach dispenser if your washer is equipped with one. Bleach clothes only in the wash cycle so the bleach can be completely removed during the rinse cycle. Hot water improves the performance of bleach.

Fabric Softeners: Fabric softeners add softness and fluffiness, reduce static electricity on synthetics so they will not cling, help decrease lint, and make pressing easier. They are available in liquid, sheet, or solid form.

Liquid fabric softener is added to the wash or rinse cycle; sheet and solid products are used in the dryer.

Read the instructions for using a fabric softener to determine at what time in the laundering cycle to add it. Dilute liquid fabric softeners with water before adding them to the automatic fabric-softener dispenser or to the rinse.

Fabric softener can stain fabric if it is poured or sprayed directly onto clothes or if it is used with a water conditioner. Sheet fabric softeners will stain polyester articles if they are used in the dryer when these fabrics are drying.

If you stain an item with fabric softener, rub the stained area with liquid detergent or a prewash spot-and-stain remover and rewash the article.

GETTING THE BEST RESULTS FROM YOUR WASHING MACHINE

Do not overload the machine; garments should not pile up past the top of the agitator.

Mix small and large items in each load for the best circulation, and distribute the load evenly around the wash basket.

Loading the washer to full capacity each time you wash will save time and energy. But don't be tempted to throw your dark bath towels in a bleach load or your sweaters in a permanent-press load just to fill it.

Add 1/2 cup vinegar to the rinse cycle of your wash to soften clothes.

The correct water temperature(s) for a load of wash varies according to the kinds of fabric being washed and the amount of soil. Use the following chart to help you.

TYPE OF LOAD	WASH TEMPERATURE	RINSE TEMPERATURE
* White and light-colored cottons and linens * Diapers * Heavily soiled permanent-press and wash-and-wear fabrics * All other greasy or heavily soiled wash	130° F.-150° F. (hot)	warm or cold
* Dark colors * Lightly and moderately soiled permanent-press and wash-and-wear fabrics * Some woven or knit synthetic fabrics (see care label) * Some washable woolens (see care label) * Any other moderately soiled wash	100° F.-110° F. (warm)	cold
* Noncolorfast fabrics * Some washable woolens (see care label) * Some woven or knit synthetic fabrics (see care label) * Fragile items * Bright colors * Any lightly soiled wash	80° F.-100° F. (cold)	cold

Use enough water to provide good circulation, but do not use so much that you waste water and energy. Most machines have a water-level control, and you should adjust this control to match each load you wash. Refer to the manufacturer's instructions for this information.

Select the type of cycle according to the kind of load and the degree of soil. Follow these guidelines, using a longer cycle for heavily soiled laundry.

TYPE OF LOAD	CYCLE
✳ Sturdy white and colorfast items	Normal
✳ Sturdy noncolorfast items	Normal
✳ Sturdy permanent-press and wash-and-wear fabrics	Permanent-press
✳ Delicate fabrics and knits	Gentle or delicate

DRY-CLEAN ONLY?

Never use vinegar on dry-clean-only fabrics. It's always a good idea to test the fabric for colorfastness before treating a stain.

Even if the tag says "dry-clean only," some items can be cleaned with a solution of 4 tablespoons baking soda in a sink of cold water. Test for colorfastness first.

WASHING BY HAND

We recommend that you never disregard the "hand wash only" label even when you're in a hurry.

Sort hand wash in the same way you sort machine wash. Separate the clothes into piles by color, putting white and light colors together, dark and noncolorfast items into separate piles.

Pretreat stains and heavily soiled areas with prewash spot-and-stain remover or by rubbing liquid detergent into the area.

Use light-duty soap or detergent and dissolve it in warm or cool wash water before adding the clothes. Submerge the articles in the water and let them soak for 3 to 5 minutes. Gently squeeze the suds through the fabric, being careful not to rub, twist, or wring excessively. Rinse articles thoroughly in cool water until the water runs clear. Add a few drops of fabric softener to the last rinse if desired.

Hang blouses, dresses, scarves, and lingerie to drip-dry. The shower is a good place for this. Use towels to blot excess moisture from sweaters, stockings, panties, and bras. Hang these items to dry only if the weight of the water will not stretch them out of shape; otherwise, dry them on a towel on a flat surface.

When washing delicate items by hand, follow garment's care instructions and add 1 or 2 tablespoons vinegar to the last rinse to help remove soap residue.

Eliminate the stale smell in stored-away hand-washables by soaking them in a solution of 4 tablespoons baking soda and 1 quart water. Rinse well, squeeze, then air-dry.

MACHINE DRYING

Shake out each article before placing it in the dryer to speed the drying time and cut down on wrinkles. Do not overload the dryer; this will cause uneven drying and excessive wrinkling.

Remove items from the dryer as soon as it stops, and hang or fold them to keep them from getting wrinkled.

Dry clothes until they are "almost dry" rather than "bone dry" if you are going to iron them.

Clean the lint filter after each use of the dryer.

Lint won't stick to your clothes while they're tumbling in the dryer if you toss in a pair of pantyhose with them.

A few tennis balls tumbling around in the dryer will be somewhat noisy...but very effective for reducing static cling. Toss them in with a load of clothes and set the dryer on low heat.

LINE DRYING

If you are going to the trouble to hang your clothes outside to dry, make sure that your clothespins and clotheslines are clean and free of rust. You can wash plastic clothespins in mild soap and warm water in an automatic clothes washer, using a mesh bag. Wash wooden clothespins in a hot dish-washing-detergent solution. Use plastic rope or plastic-coated wire for your clothesline, and wipe it with a damp cloth before using it.

* Attach items to the clothesline by their most sturdy edges.
* Smooth the clothes as you hang them, running your fingers down seams and along the front, collar, and cuff edges. Dry white and light-colored items in the sun and bright-colored items in the shade.
* Hang pants by the cuffs and let their weight reduce wrinkles.
* Cut the fingers off a pair of cotton gloves, then slip the "fingers" over the arms of a weathered clothespin. They'll prevent marks on your clothes.
* Drop a spoon into each leg of a pair of pantyhose or another thin garment to keep them from wrapping around the clothesline on a windy day.
* Bring in clothes as soon as they dry. Bright sun and extreme cold can weaken fibers.

TROUBLESHOOTING: YELLOWED FABRIC AND DYE PROBLEMS

* If your good ol' black cotton T-shirts have faded to dark brown or eggplant from frequent washings, add 1 cup strong Lipton tea to the rinse cycle next time. They'll be restored to their original glory.

* Whiten yellowed linens by dropping 1 or 2 denture cleanser tablets in a tub of warm water and soaking the fabric overnight.

* Any colored clothing item that has dulled can be brightened by soaking it in 1 gallon warm water and 1 cup vinegar. Follow this with a clear water rinse.

* Boil yellowed cotton or linen fabrics in a mixture of water, 1 tablespoon salt, and 1/4 cup baking soda. Soak for 1 hour, then launder as usual.

* Bleach soiled handkerchiefs by soaking them for a few hours in a solution of warm water and 1 tablespoon cream of tartar. Soak especially dingy hankies for about an hour in a sink of water with 1 tablespoon cream of tartar and 2 teaspoons Tide laundry detergent. Wash as usual.

* If you just can't get those dingy whites clean, don't discard them. Strong, hot Lipton tea is the perfect dye for natural-fiber fabric or yarn. Soak the material until it is a shade darker than desired (as it dries, it becomes lighter). Rinse in clear, cold water; allow to air-dry.

* Herbal teas can also dye fabrics. Go bold or subtle as you use, for example, hibiscus for red tones or licorice for soft brown. Always experiment on fabric scraps to get the results you want.

TROUBLESHOOTING: STAINS

* Equal parts bleach and milk can take stains out of old linens. Make a small quantity of the solution, dip a cotton ball in it, and gently dab the stains. When the spots are gone, launder as usual. This treatment also works on discoloration lines that form on the folds of long-stored linens.

* For tough stains, including mildew, make a thin paste of lemon juice and salt. Apply to the stain, set the item in the sun to dry, then wash as usual.

* Here's another method to get rid of mildew: A mixture of salt, distilled white vinegar, and water should remove mildew stains on most fabrics. Use up to full-strength vinegar if mildew is extensive.

* To remove a food stain (whether fresh or dried-on) from a washable item of clothing, use club soda. First, blot the spill by pressing lightly with a paper towel. Then sponge the fabric with club soda and launder as usual.

* Remove a wine spill from cotton fabric by immediately sprinkling stained area with enough salt to soak up liquid. Soak fabric for 1 hour in cold water, then launder as usual.

* A red wine stain yields to club soda. If the spot is still wet, blot it with a paper towel. Pour on a generous amount of club soda; rub gently with another paper towel or a sponge. Repeat if necessary.

* To remove tough juice stains, dilute lemon juice or distilled white vinegar with water. Soak the stain in this solution, then wash as usual.

* Brand-new coffee or tea drips should be removed easily with lots of cold water on a damp cloth (if fabric is not dry-clean only). For coffee or tea stains that have set, soak item in a solution of 1 part vinegar and 2 parts water, then hang in the sun to dry.

* Those hard-to-fix bleach spots on clothes might be fixable with a crayon. Pick a matching color, warm the fabric with an iron, and color the spot. Cover it with wax paper and iron on low to set the color.

* To remove a bloodstain, dampen the area with water and rub with baking soda. Follow by dabbing with hydrogen peroxide until the stain is gone. Test for colorfastness first.

* You can also get rid of a bloodstain by applying a paste of cornstarch and water to the stain right away. Let dry, then brush off. Repeat if necessary. This works on clothing and linens.

* Clean a fresh bloodstain with hydrogen peroxide. Dab on the peroxide, then blot off, repeating as necessary. Test a hidden area first to be sure the fabric is colorfast.

* A fresh bloodstain should disappear easily if it is immediately covered with salt and blotted with cold water. Keep adding fresh water and blotting until stain is gone.

* Chocolate stains melt away in the face of undiluted ammonia. Scrub the stained area, then wash as usual.

* Revive grass-stained clothes or sneakers with molasses. Rub a little molasses into any stains; let sit overnight. Wash item with a mild soap—not laundry detergent.

* Remove severe grass stains from white clothes by soaking in undiluted vinegar for a half hour before washing.

* Rub baking soda into polyester fabrics to remove a grease spot. Brush off, and the stain should be gone.

* A grease stain can sometimes be removed by rubbing baby powder or cornstarch into it. Allow the powder or corn starch to sit for an hour or more to soak up the grease, then brush off and wash as usual. If stain remains, repeat until it's gone.

* To remove a fresh grease spill on fabric, cover with salt or corn meal and allow it to absorb as much of the mess as possible. Repeat until spot is gone. Brush off and launder.

* Double-knit fabrics can be a special stain challenge when it comes to grease. Add 1/2 teaspoon salt to a small dish of ammonia and dab mixture directly onto grease spot. Let sit, then wash as usual.

* Try covering a fresh gravy stain with salt and letting it absorb as much of the grease as possible. A stubborn stain may require dabbing and blotting with a solution of equal parts ammonia and vinegar until it disappears.

* Pour Pepsi or club soda directly on a grease spot. Let it sit for a few minutes to loosen the stain, then wash as usual.

* Remove grease from suede by dipping a cloth in vinegar and gently sponging stain. Let dry completely, then use a fine brush to restore nap in suede.

* Clean suede with baking soda applied with a soft brush. Let it sit, then brush it off.

* Remove an ink stain from leather by laying the item flat and sprinkling baking soda on the stain. Leave on until ink is absorbed, brush off, and repeat if necessary.

* Ink stains or scuff marks on suede clothing or shoes can be removed, or at least minimized, with fine-grit 3M sandpaper. Sand with a light touch, then use an old Reach toothbrush or a nailbrush to restore the nap afterward.

* A lipstick stain on silk sounds like an automatic bill from the dry cleaner. Try this method instead. Place a piece of clear tape or masking tape on the spot, then pull it off. If some of the lipstick remains, sprinkle on some baby powder or crushed chalk. With a clean cloth, dab until both the powder and the lipstick vanish.

* Oil stain got you stumped? Dip a wedge of lime in salt and rub the spot. Launder as usual.

* Conquer rust stains with this treatment. Wet the stained area with lemon juice; hold it directly over the steam from a pot of boiling water for a few minutes. Rinse well.

* Make a thin paste of distilled white vinegar and salt and spread paste on a rust stain in fabric. Lay item out in the sun to bleach it. Alternatively, apply paste, stretch fabric over a large kettle, and pour boiling water through stained area. In both cases, allow item to dry, then check stain. Run item through the rinse cycle in your washing machine and check stain again. Repeat treatment if any stain remains.

* To remove a rust mark on fabric, dampen the spot and rub cream of tartar into it. Wait 1 hour, then wash as usual. Repeat if necessary.

* Those yellow stains in the armpits and around the collars of your favorite white T-shirts aren't a sign that you're sweating too much or not cleaning properly. These areas are just harder to get clean and are made up of more than just old perspiration and dirt. Plus, if you have hard water, the deodorant residue (and soap and perspiration) won't wash out properly. Here's one method for attacking these problem stains: Mix 1

quart water with 4 tablespoons salt. Sponge this mixture onto stained areas; repeat until stains disappear. Launder as usual.

✳ Aspirin can remove perspiration stains from white fabrics. Dissolve 2 tablets in 1/2 cup of warm water and apply to the stain. Let it sit for about 2 hours before laundering.

✳ For perspiration stains, scrub on a paste of baking soda and water; let sit for 1 hour, then launder as usual.

✳ Try soaking white shirts and T-shirts in undiluted vinegar to get rid of yellow stains in the armpits and around the collar. Let the item sit in the vinegar for 15 to 20 minutes, then launder as usual.

✳ Treat stubborn perspiration stains around the collar with a paste of 4 tablespoons baking soda and 1/4 cup water. Rub in, add a little distilled white vinegar to the collar, and wash.

✳ Remove candle wax from fabric such as clothing or table linens by putting a paper towel or a brown paper bag over the spot. Press with an iron on a low heat setting (keep the iron in one place) for several seconds. The wax will be absorbed by the paper and the iron will remain clean.

✳ Clean leather with a mixture of 1 cup boiled linseed oil and 1 cup vinegar. Carefully apply to any spots with a soft cloth. Let dry.

✳ A toothbrush is a wonderful laundry-day tool. To remove dried stains, put the garment on a flat surface, hold a piece of paper next to the stain, and gently brush the dried material onto the paper. Some stains, such as dried mud, are removed completely; others will have some residue that should come out during the regular wash cycle.

Doing your laundry isn't the only thing you can do to maintain your clothes. In this section we'll discuss some easy ways and quick fixes that will help your clothes last longer.

CLOTHING

* When you buy a new garment, dab the center of each button with clear nail enamel to seal the threads. The buttons will stay on longer.

* Put a stop to a run in your pantyhose by dabbing the ends of the run with clear nail enamel.

* Paint the edges of a fraying garment with clear nail enamel.

* Keep buckles from chipping or tarnishing by painting them with clear nail enamel. This also helps keep buckles shiny.

* Put a dab of clear nail enamel over the knot on a small ribbon to keep it from coming untied.

* To attach buttons more securely, sew them on with dental floss instead of thread. Just color the floss with a matching marker or crayon.

* Using a Q-tips cotton swab, apply a bit of extra virgin olive oil to the teeth of a stuck zipper. Slowly work the tab down until it's free.

* You can replace a missing zipper tab with a paper clip or a safety pin. Dress it up with a piece of ribbon or yarn or a dollop of paint.

* Fix a falling hem in a pinch with a length of duct tape. The tape is especially suited for heavy fabrics such as denim.

* You're all dressed up. You do have someplace to go. Unfortunately, you also have pet hair and lint on your outfit, and there's no lint remover in sight. Not to worry. Grab a roll of duct tape and cut a strip of tape about 5 inches long. Wrap it around your hand, adhesive side out, and roll it over your clothing until all the offending particles are gone. Make sure you aren't wiping the tape across the fabric; on some garments, it may mess up the nap.

* A rip in your ski pants or jacket can leave you cold, quite literally. Don't panic or pay exorbitant prices in the lodge shop to replace the item; just cut a length of duct tape a bit longer than the rip. Position the tape inside the rip, sticky side out. Join the two sides of the ripped fabric so they meet in the middle. Carefully press onto the tape.

ACCESSORIES

* Need a place to store your belts? Roll them up and place them in an empty coffee can. (Tip: A clear lid will make it easy to find the right belt.) These containers will keep your belts from creasing, and the easy access won't "waist" your time.

* Neatly store scarves in a dresser drawer using empty cores from rolls of toilet tissue or paper towels (cut in half). Stand them up in the drawer and tuck a folded scarf into each one.

IN YOUR CLOSET

* Preserve space in your closet by hanging your scarves through plastic six-pack rings from soda cans. Attach the rings to a hanger using twist ties or clear tape.

* If a good pair of pants has been in the closet, on a regular hanger, for a while, there's likely an obvious, ugly crease from the hanger. Next time, cut an old paper towel tube lengthwise and place it over the bottom of the hanger. (Cut the ends of the tube to shorten if necessary.) Tape the tube back together to make sure it doesn't fall off the hanger. Hang your pants over the protective tube—good-bye, creases!

* Garments falling off their hangers? Before you hang a garment, put a rubber band on each end of the hanger.

* To keep spaghetti straps from slipping off wire hangers, use paper clips to attach them.

JEWELRY CARE

* Don't let it go down the drain: When cleaning your good jewelry, put a tea strainer over the sink drain.

* Dissolve 2 Alka-Seltzer tablets in a glass of water and use to soak dull or tarnished jewelry. Let soak for only 2 minutes, then rub dry.

* Extra virgin olive oil and vegetable oil each make a good cleaner for pearls. Just dab a little of either on each pearl, then wipe dry with a soft cloth.

* To clean a diamond ring, use Crest toothpaste on an old toothbrush. Scrub gently, rinse, dry, and step back to enjoy the sparkle!

* Use denture cleanser tablets dissolved in a glass of water to make your diamonds sparkle. Just drop jewelry in the solution for 2 minutes.

* Soak your gems, precious or semiprecious, in a glass of club soda overnight. In the morning, they'll sparkle and shine.

* Does a ring discolor your finger? Apply clear nail enamel to the inside of the band.

* Keep it clean: Prevent your silver jewelry and your costume jewelry from tarnishing by putting a stick of chalk in the jewelry box.

* Does your jewelry box look as if the chains have been wrestling with each other? Solve that problem by dropping each chain through the end of a drinking straw that's been cut in half. Fasten the clasp on the outside of the straw.

* Untangling a fine gold or silver chain can seem hopeless. Try setting the chain on a piece of cling wrap and putting a small drop of baby oil on the knot. Using 2 sewing needles, gently work apart the knot. Wash with water and a little Dawn dishwashing liquid; rinse and dry well.

BEAT SPOTS & STAINS

When you walk into some homes, it's like entering an archaeological site: faint crayon marks on the wallpaper record the toddler age, grease spots on the carpet in front of the door to the garage recall the period of do-it-yourself car maintenance, and the discolored spots on the living room carpet will never forget Fido. Most of us don't want our houses to say quite so much about us. We'll help you deal with the unusual and not-so-unusual spots and stains that find their way onto your carpeting, your clothes, your furniture, and the other surfaces in your home. Each stain requires its own special treatment, or you may end up with a worse mess than you started with. We want to share with you some basic information about stains and stain-removal. We'll give you a comprehensive shopping list of cleaning tools and products that you will want to have in your stain-removal kit to combat stains, and we'll teach you the eight basic techniques of stain-removal.

THREE KINDS OF STAINS

Greasy Stains: You can sometimes remove grease spots from washable fabrics by laundering. Pretreating by rubbing detergent directly into the spot often helps, as does using dry-cleaning solution on the stain. If you are treating an old stain or one that has been ironed, a yellow stain may remain after treatment with a solvent. Bleach can sometimes remove this yellow residue.

To remove grease spots from nonwashable fabrics, sponge the stain with dry-cleaning solution. Elimination of the stain may require several applications. Allow the spot to dry completely between spongings. Greasy stains may also be removed from nonwashable fabrics by using an absorbent, such as cornstarch, cornmeal, French chalk, or fuller's earth (mineral clay available at most drug stores). Dust the absorbent on the greasy spot. When it begins to look caked, it should be shaken or brushed off.

Absorbents are easy to use and will not harm fabrics. However, other stain-removal agents, such as detergents, dry-cleaning solvents, and bleach, can damage fibers. Before using any of these products, you should carefully read the care label on the stained item and the label on the product container. If you do not have either one of these labels, we recommend that you test the cleaning product on the fabric in an inconspicuous area.

Nongreasy Stains: Fruit juice on your collar, black coffee on your lapel, tea on your pocket flap, food coloring on your cuff, ink on your pant leg—nongreasy stains are easy to acquire, but not impossible to remove. If you are treating a nongreasy stain on a washable fabric, we recommend that you sponge the stain with cool water as soon as possible.

If this doesn't remove the stain, try soaking the fabric in cool water. The stain may soak out within half an hour, or you may need to leave the item in water overnight.

If some of the stain still remains after this treatment, try gently rubbing liquid detergent into it, then rinse with cool water. The very last resort is to use bleach, but always read the fabric-care label before you bleach. If the stain is old or has already been ironed, it may be impossible to remove it completely.

A nongreasy stain on fabric that cannot be washed can be sponged with cool water. Place an absorbent pad under the stained area and slowly drip water through the fabric with an eye dropper or pump/trigger spray bottle. This method of flushing the stain lets you control the amount of water and the rate at which it flows through the fabric so that you don't inadvertently spread the stain.

If you treat a nongreasy stain with water while it is still fresh, you often can remove it entirely. If water alone fails to remove the stain, work liquid detergent into the stain and rinse it by sponging or flushing with cool water. Sponge the spot with rubbing alcohol after you've rinsed it to remove detergent residue and to speed drying. (**Caution:** If you're treating acetate, acrylic, modacrylic, rayon, triacetate, or vinyl, be sure to dilute the alcohol with water, 1 part alcohol to 2 parts water.)

Combination Stains: Some stains are double trouble. Coffee with cream, Thousand Island salad dressing, and lipstick leave a trail of combination stains behind them; they're both greasy and nongreasy. Getting rid of combination stains is a two-part operation. First get rid of the nongreasy stain and then attack the greasy residue. On most fabrics, you'll need to sponge the stain with cool water, then work liquid detergent into the stain and rinse thoroughly. After the fabric has dried, apply dry-cleaning solution to the greasy part of the stain. Allow the fabric to dry.

TAKING THE STRESS OUT OF STAINS

There's a surefire strategy for beating stains. You'll save time by doing it right the first time rather than wasting time experimenting with various cures for the problem and possibly making the stain worse than it was to start with. Here are the basic rules.

* The quicker the better. The best time to treat a stain is the moment after it occurs. The longer it sets, the more likely it is that a stain will become permanent.
* Know what you're cleaning. Identify both the staining agent and the stained surface. Both will affect the way in which you treat the stain.
* Clean it off before you clean it. Remove as much of the staining agent as you possibly can before you begin the stain-removal process.
* Be gentle. Rubbing, folding, wringing, and squeezing cause stains to penetrate more deeply and may damage delicate fibers.
* Keep it cool. Avoid using hot water, high-heat clothes dryers, and irons on stains; heat makes some stains impossible to remove.
* Pretest stain removers. Even clear water can damage some fabrics, so test every cleaner you plan to use in an inconspicuous place before you use it on the stain.
* Follow directions. Read manufacturers' care labels and directions on product containers before you start to clean a stain.
* Work from the edges into the center. You won't spread the stain or leave a ring.

YOUR STAIN REMOVAL KIT

To beat stains, you have to be prepared. Your well-stocked stain-removal kit, like a first-aid kit, should be ready to help you handle cleaning emergencies whenever they occur.

Here are the tools you'll need to have in your kit: clean, white cotton cloths; disposable diapers for absorbing flushed cleaning solutions; white blotting paper; white paper toweling; a spoon, blunt knife, or spatula for scraping; an eyedropper or trigger spray bottle; a small brush; several colorfast weights

Your kit will also need to include a variety of stain-removal agents. What you need depends on what you are likely to have to clean. You will be able to purchase most of them at your local hardware store, grocery store, or pharmacy.

Absorbents "soak up" grease stains. We consider cornmeal the best absorbent for light colors, and fuller's earth the best for dark colors. Spread the absorbent on the stained areas and allow it to work. As the grease is soaked up, the absorbent material will cake or become gummy. It should then be shaken or brushed off. You should repeat the process until the stain has been removed. This may take as long as eight hours or more.

Bleaching Agents, Chlorine: Commonly used to bleach white cotton, linen, and synthetic fabrics, chlorine bleach is a powerful stain remover, which can weaken fibers if it is allowed to stay on fabric for too long a time. Never use chlorine bleach on silk, wool, or fabrics that are exposed to sunlight, such as curtains. Always test chlorine bleach in an inconspicuous place before bleaching an entire item.

Caution: Chlorine bleach is poisonous. If it comes in contact with skin or eyes, it will cause burns and irritation.

Bleaching Agents, Color Removers: Hydrosulfite, the active chemical compound in color removers, lightens the color of fabric before it is redyed a lighter color. This chemical also removes some stains from colorfast fibers. Always pretest color remover. If the product causes a distinct color change instead of fading the fabric, you may be able to restore the original color by rinsing immediately with cool water. If the color fades when color remover is applied, the original color cannot be restored. Color remover should not be used in a metal container. **Caution:** Color removers are poisonous. Avoid prolonged contact with skin. Observe all precautions on the label.

Bleaching Agents, Hydrogen Peroxide: The 3-percent solution of hydrogen peroxide that is sold as a mild antiseptic is a safe bleach for most fibers. A stronger solution used for lightening hair is too strong to use on fabric and other household surfaces. Buy peroxide in small quantities and store it in a cool, dark place; it loses strength quickly after it is opened and if it is exposed to light.

Chemical, Acetic acid: You can buy acetic acid in a 10-percent solution at pharmacies. White vinegar is a 5-percent acetic acid and can be used as a substitute for the stronger solution. Acetic acid is a clear fluid, used full strength to remove stains on silk and wool. It must be diluted with 2 parts water for use on cotton and linen. (We recommend that you test for colorfastness.) Never use this chemical on acetate. If acetic acid causes a color change, try sponging the affected areas with ammonia; this may restore the color.

Chemical, Acetone: Fingernail-polish remover and household-cement thinner are acetone based, but they should not be substituted for pure acetone because they contain other ingredients that may worsen the stain. You can purchase acetone at pharmacies and paint stores. The colorless liquid smells like peppermint, and it can be used on stains caused by substances such as fingernail polish or household cement. Although acetone will damage neither natural fibers nor most synthetics, it should be tested to make sure that dyed fabrics will not be harmed. Acetone should not be used on fabrics containing acetate; it will dissolve them. Caution: Acetone is flammable and evaporates rapidly, producing toxic fumes. When using acetone, work outside or in a well-ventilated area. Avoid inhaling the fumes. Store acetone in a tightly capped container in a cool place.

Chemical, Alcohol: Isopropyl alcohol in a 70-percent solution is sufficient for most stain-removal jobs that call for alcohol. Stronger, denatured alcohol (90-percent solution) can also be used. Be sure you do not buy alcohol with added color or fragrance. Since alcohol will fade some dyes, we recommend that you test it on the fabric you will be cleaning. Alcohol will damage acetate, triacetate, modacrylic, and acrylic fibers. If you must use it on fibers in the acetate family, dilute the alcohol with 2 parts water. **Caution:** Alcohol is poisonous and flammable.

Chemical, Ammonia: Use plain household ammonia without added color or fragrance for stain removal. Because ammonia affects some dyes, we recommend that you test it on the stained article. To restore color changed by ammonia, rinse the affected area in water and apply a few drops of white vinegar, then rinse with clear water. Ammonia damages silk and wool; if you must use it on these fibers, dilute it with an equal amount of water and use as sparingly as possible. **Caution:** Ammonia is poisonous. Avoid inhaling its fumes. It will cause burns or irritation if it comes in contact with skin or eyes.

Chemical, Coconut Oil: You can buy coconut oil in drug and health-food stores. It is used in the preparation of dry spotter that is used to remove many kinds of stains. If you cannot obtain coconut oil, you may substitute mineral oil, which is almost as effective. To make dry spotter, combine 1 part coconut oil and 8 parts liquid dry-cleaning solvent. Store this solution in a tightly capped container to prevent evaporation.

Chemical, Glycerine: Use glycerine in the preparation of wet spotter that is used to remove many kinds of stains. To make wet spotter, mix 1 part glycerine, 1 part white dishwashing detergent, and 8 parts water. Store the solution in a plastic squeeze bottle, and shake well before each use.

Chemical, Oxalic Acid: Effective in treating ink and rust stains, oxalic acid crystals are sold in many pharmacies. The crystals must be dissolved in water (1 tablespoon crystals to 1 cup warm water). Test the solution on a hidden corner of the spotted item before using it on the stain. Moisten the stained area with the solution. Allow it to dry, then reapply. Be sure all traces of the solution are rinsed out. Caution: Oxalic acid is poisonous. Avoid contact with skin and eyes, and wear rubber gloves when working with this chemical.

Chemical, Turpentine: Most often used as a thinner for oil-based paints, turpentine is effective on paint and grease stains. **Caution:** Turpentine is flammable and poisonous. Observe all the precautions stated on the label.

Chemical, Vinegar: When using vinegar on a stain, always use white (clear) vinegar. Cider and red-wine vinegar have color that can leave a stain. Vinegar is a 5-percent acetic acid solution and should be diluted if you use it on cotton or linen. Vinegar is safe for all other colorfast fibers, but it can change the color of some dyes, so always test it on an inconspicuous area first. If an article changes color, rinse the affected area with water to which you've added a few drops of ammonia. Rinse thoroughly with clear water. This may restore the color.

Washing Agents, Detergents: When stain-removal directions call for a mild detergent, choose a white dishwashing liquid; the dyes in nonwhite detergents may worsen the stain. When instructions call for a pretreating paste made of detergent and water, use a powdered detergent that does not contain bleach. When the stain-removal directions specify that you should apply a liquid laundry detergent directly to the spot or stain, be sure to read the directions on the product's label carefully. Some products cannot safely be used in this manner. Other detergent products, such as those used in automatic dishwashers or for heavy-duty household cleaning, and certain laundry products may contain alkalies. They can set stains caused by ammonia, soap, and oven cleaner and should not be used for spot removal.

Washing Agents, Enzyme Presoaks: Most effective on protein stains, such as those caused by meat juices, eggs, and blood, enzyme presoaks may harm silk and wool. Make sure you have exhausted every alternative before you use enzyme presoaks on these two fabrics. Use a presoak as soon as possible after mixing with water; enzyme-presoak solutions become inactive in storage. Be sure to read and observe all the directions on the product label.

Washing Agents, Powdered Cleansers: Scouring powders and baking soda can be used to remove stains on surfaces that will not be harmed by abrasives. However, you should be aware that prolonged or overly vigorous scrubbing with these products can scratch even the most durable surface. Make sure you rinse away all the powder when the job is completed.

Washing Agents, Pretreaters: Use pretreaters on spots and stains when you think that a stain might not respond to normal laundering procedures. Pretreaters start the cleaning process before the stained item is put in the washer. They must be used in conjunction with the rest of the laundering process; do not try to use a pretreater alone, as though it were a spot remover. After applying a pretreater, you should not allow the fabric to dry out before you begin washing.

Washing Agents, Soaps: Bath soaps with added moisturizers, fragrance, dyes, or deodorant should not be used to treat spots. Purchase either laundry soap or pure white soap.

SAFETY PRECAUTIONS

In order to treat stains and spots as soon as they occur, you have to be prepared. But many of the products you stock in your stain-removal kit are flammable or toxic, and certain safety tips should be kept in mind when storing and using these products.

✳ Store stain-removing products carefully and out of the reach of children. The storage area should be cool, dry, and separate from food storage areas. Keep bottles tightly capped and boxes closed.

✳ Do not transfer cleaning products to new containers. Keep them in their original containers so that you never have to search for directions for their proper use and so that they are always clearly labeled.

✳ Follow the directions on the product label and heed all warnings.

✳ Glass and unchipped porcelain containers are preferable to metal or plastic when working with stain-removal agents. Never use plastic with solvents. Never use any container that is rusty. Clean all containers thoroughly after use.

✳ Protect your hands with rubber gloves. Don't touch your eyes or skin while handling stain-removal chemicals. If you do accidentally touch your eyes or spill chemicals on your skin, flush immediately with clear water.

✳ Remember that the fumes of solvents are toxic; work in a well-ventilated area.

✳ Do not use chemicals near an open flame or electrical outlet. Do not smoke while using chemicals.

✳ Do not use a solvent as a laundry additive.

✳ When using a solvent on a washable fabric, be sure to rinse all traces of the solvent out of the fabric.

✳ Do not experiment with mixtures of stain-removal agents. Never combine products unless specifically directed to do so in the recipes for homemade cleaning solutions in this book. Many combinations can be dangerous.

✳   If the cleaning process requires the use of more than one stain-removal agent, rinse out each product thoroughly before applying the next.

EIGHT WAYS TO BEAT STAINS

We would all like to be able to squirt a little dab of the right solution on a stain, stand back, and watch the spot fade away forever. Unfortunately, stain removal has not yet become quite that simple. But can beat the stain with a combination of the right techniques and the right cleaning solutions. We have already discussed the cleaning supplies you need to have on hand in your stain-removal kit, but you also need to know how these tools and products are used to remove stains quickly and effectively.

There are eight basic techniques for stain removal: brushing, flushing, freezing, presoaking, pretreating, scraping, sponging, and tamping. The right technique for a particular spot or stain depends on what was spilled and where it fell.

Use **brushing** to remove dried stains. Some kinds of spots, such as dried mud, can be removed completely by brushing. For other kinds of stains, brushing is only a step in the cleaning process.

We recommend a small, stiff-bristled brush for this technique. When you're working on fabric, stretch the piece on a firm, clean surface. Hold a sheet of paper next to the stain, and brush the staining material onto the paper. A gentle motion with the brush pulls the stain up off the surface and onto the paper.

Use **flushing** to remove loosened staining materials and the residue from stain-removal agents. If cleaning products are left in the material, they may cause additional staining or even damage the treated article.

When you are flushing a stain, especially one on nonwashable fabric, you need to control the flow of water carefully so that you don't spread the stain or get the fabric wetter than you need to. An eyedropper or a trigger spray bottle that can be adjusted to a fine stream lets you precisely control the amount of liquid flushed through the fabric. Before you begin this treatment, place a clean absorbent pad, such as a disposable diaper, under the spot. Then slowly and carefully apply water or the

recommended stain remover to the stain. Work slowly so that you don't flood the pad with more liquid than it can absorb. Replace the absorbent pad frequently to prevent the deposited staining material from restaining the fabric. If you're treating a stain on a washable fabric, rinse the article in warm water after you have flushed the stain.

Candle wax, chewing gum, and other gooey substances are easier to remove when they are cold and hard. Hold an ice cube against the stain to **freeze** it. If the stained item is not washable, place the ice in a plastic bag. You can put a small stained item in a plastic bag and place the whole thing in the freezer. After the stain has solidified, it can usually be gently lifted or scraped from the surface.

When your wash is grayed, yellowed, or heavily soiled, washing alone will not get it clean and bright— you will have to **presoak.** Sort the soiled items before presoaking; items that are not colorfast should be presoaked separately from colorfast items because their colors may bleed.

You may add bleach, laundry detergent, or an enzyme presoak to the soaking water. But don't use chlorine bleach and an enzyme product at the same time. You can leave colorfast, stained articles in a presoak for as long as it takes to get them clean, but for most stains, 30 minutes is long enough. Items that aren't colorfast should be soaked only briefly.

Before you wash a load of presoaked laundry, make sure that it has been thoroughly rinsed and that no residue of the presoak is left on the items.

Pretreat oily, greasy stains with liquid laundry detergent, a soil-and-spot-removing spray, bar soap, or a pretreating paste made from powdered detergent and water. After you apply a pre-treater, rub it into the stain gently, and wash the item as you would normally.

Scrape away solid staining material with a dull knife, spoon, or spatula before you apply stain remover. Don't press too hard; move the edge of your scraping tool back and forth across the stain in short strokes.

Put an absorbent pad, such as a disposable diaper, under the stain before you **sponge** it. On a carpet you will have to work without an absorbent pad, so be especially careful not to use excessive amounts of cleaning solution or water. Use another pad or a sponge to apply the stain-removing agent.

Sponge the stain gently using light strokes. Change either pad as soon as any of the stain is deposited on it.

Some fabrics, such as acetate, triacetate, and rayon, are likely to develop rings when they are sponged. When you work on stains on these fabrics, barely wet the pad with stain remover and touch the fabric lightly so that the stain remover is absorbed as slowly as possible. Blot the treated area between absorbent pads. Allow it to air-dry. Ironing or drying with heat may cause the stain remover itself to stain the fabric.

The best way to get some stains out of durable, tightly woven fabrics is to **tamp** them with a soft-bristled brush. Place the stained article on a hard work surface, not on a pad, and lightly rap the stain with the tips of the bristles. Repeat until the stain is removed. Use this technique rarely, because tamping will harm most fabrics.

Many of us who are otherwise quite tidy treat our cars as though they were traveling dustbins. In the backseat, the debris from fast-food meals gets piled on top of autumn leaves, comic books, broken toys, and you name it. The outside of the car has an allover greasy film of road dirt and mud spatters on the fenders. The car already looks like a clunker, and you're still paying for it.

Cleaning and maintaining the original appearance of your car may not be high on your list of favorite ways to spend your weekend, but we've found that it is time well spent. You can expect to obtain more at trade-in time or when you sell your car if you've helped your car to keep its good looks. Your car is a very large investment, and keeping it looking as new as possible protects that investment. In this section, we'll show you how to clean your car-inside and out.

CARPETS

Keeping the carpet in your car clean is almost impossible: There's no place to wipe your feet before you get in. Mats offer some protection from dirt and grime, and we suggest that you install them in a new car as soon as you buy it and replace them when they become worn. But even when you use mats to protect the carpeting, dirt and grime inevitably accumulate in the carpet fibers.

Vacuum the carpeting in your car frequently to remove the grit and soil that can break down carpet fibers and cause unnecessary wear. A handheld cordless vacuum is especially good for vacuuming your car, and its recharging stand can be mounted right in your garage so it's conveniently at hand. Every time you vacuum the car, remove the mats, shake them thoroughly, and vacuum them as well.

Spills in the car are not like spills in the house. When you turn a corner too fast and spill your morning coffee, you can't stop in the middle of traffic and clean up the mess. But you should try to wipe up spills soon after they occur. Keep paper towels and a whisk broom in the car and accessible for emergency cleanups.

Make it your habit to roll up your car windows whenever you park your car outside. If rain or water from the neighbor's lawn sprinkler leaks into your car and soaks the carpet, it is difficult to dry it out, and mildew can set in quickly.

When the carpeting in your car needs to be cleaned, use a spray or spray-foam carpet cleaner. Some manufacturers make carpet-cleaning products especially for cars. Read and follow the instructions for the best results. Vacuum the carpet after cleaning only when it is completely dry.

Salt residues can be removed from carpets with a solution made of equal parts vinegar and water. Apply the mixture with a sponge, but do not overwet the carpeting. Allow the carpet to dry thoroughly, then vacuum.

CHROME

Shiny chrome adds sparkle to a car's appearance, and chrome must be cleaned and polished regularly to prevent rust and corrosion. Polish chrome after the car has been washed. Remove rust spots with a steel-wool pad or a piece of crumpled aluminum foil. Wax chrome trim when you wax the car's body. Use a different cloth to polish the chrome than you use for the body.

Residues of salt will pit chrome. Have your car washed frequently during the winter when the roads have been salted, and hose off salt residues when the temperature is above freezing.

Many commercial chrome cleaners and polishes are available. If you use one, follow the manufacturer's instructions for the best results.

CHROME CLEANER

Dip a moistened sponge into baking soda and rub onto the chrome. Let it sit for a minute, then rinse, and buff the chrome dry with a soft cloth. Use a synthetic scouring pad with the soda for particularly stubborn spots.

FLOOR MATS

Rubber mats give your automobile's carpet essential protection from excessive wear. Clean the mats every time you wash your car. Even though it may take a bit of extra effort, you should clean car mats frequently in the winter, because they accumulate salt and sand when it's snowy. Use a stiff-bristled brush and scrub them with a detergent solution. Do not use harsh chemicals, solvents, or steel wool to clean the mats; these cleaners will damage the rubber. After washing the mats, apply a rubber protectant or liquid-wax shoe polish.

FLOOR-MAT CLEANER

Mix 3 tablespoons mild dish washing detergent in 1 gallon warm water. Gently scrub the mats until all the dirt and grime has been removed. Allow the mats to dry thoroughly on both sides before replacing them in your car.

PAINT

Drive-through car washes are convenient and many use the proper techniques to clean and protect a car's finish. But some use strong detergents that can eventually ruin the finish. Washing your car yourself is a safe alternative to high-priced car washes. You can achieve professional results by washing, drying, and waxing your car by hand with the right equipment and methods.

Move your car to a shaded spot; washing or waxing a car in the hot sun or when the surface is hot may cause streaking and may damage the finish.

Close all the car windows tightly before starting to wash your car. Then thoroughly hose off the dust and loose dirt; brushing it off with a cloth or even with your hand may scratch the finish. Use a garden nozzle on the hose that provides strong water pressure. Spray the wheels, hubcaps, undersurface of the fenders (avoid wetting the engine compartment), bumpers, and as far under the chassis as possible, using a hard stream of water to remove dirt, mud, and salt.

We recommend that you use mild dishwashing liquid or commercial car shampoo to clean your car. Remember that you are using cold water and will need to use plenty of detergent. Apply the cleaning solution with a clean, soft sponge, mitt, or cloth, scrubbing lightly where necessary. Work from the top down. Wash one area at a time, but keep water running over the entire car so that the dirt slides off rather than being scrubbed in.

Use a cleaner, automotive rubbing compound, or cleaner/wax on older cars to help remove the oxidized layer. Remove tar deposits with special tar remover. You can also remove tar, as well as bird droppings and insects, with a cloth saturated with vegetable oil. Hold the cloth on the dirty area until the material lifts off with gentle rubbing. Rinse the car before the suds dry. You may have to work quickly to do this on hot days and in dry climates.

Dry the car with a soft, absorbent terry-cloth towel or a chamois to prevent water spots. Paper toweling can scratch automobile finishes. It should not be used to dry the exterior of the car except the windows.

When water no longer beads up on the car's surface, apply wax or polish, following the manu-facturer's instructions. After the wax has dried, sprinkle baking soda or cornstarch on the surface. Either powder will pick up the wax and help bring out surface luster. If dried wax remains around the chrome trim, remove it with a soft-bristled brush.

TIRES

Wash tires and hubcaps after the rest of the car has been washed. Hose them with a hard stream of water to remove loose dirt before scrubbing.

Use a special tire brush or a sponge to remove soil and pebbles from the tires and the spokes of the hubcaps. Tires can be cleaned with all-purpose cleaners, steel-wool soap pads, and special whitewall cleaners. A synthetic scouring pad should be used to remove black scuff marks from whitewalls. Alloy hubcaps must be treated especially gently because their surfaces are easily damaged.

Coat the cleaned tires with a rubber protectant to help maintain a shiny appearance and to minimize rubber deterioration. Self-polishing floor wax will also make tires shine.

CLOTH UPHOLSTERY

Care should be taken to avoid spots and spills on cloth upholstery because it is not easy to clean. Mop up all spills as soon as possible, and spot treat them to avoid stains. Always carry paper toweling in your car to absorb spills.

Vacuum cloth upholstery, using a cordless vacuum or the upholstery brush attachment. We recommend that you use a crevice tool to pick up dirt from hard-to-reach places.

Any commercial upholstery shampoo can be used to clean automobile upholstery. Follow the manufacturer's instructions, and vacuum thoroughly when the product is completely dry.

MAKE IT YOURSELF!

UPHOLSTERY CLEANER

Make a stiff foam by mixing ¼ cup white liquid dish washing detergent in 1 cup warm water and beating the mixture with an eggbeater. Spread the foam over the upholstery with a sponge, using circular, overlapping strokes. Let it dry, then vacuum the soil away.

VINYL & LEATHER UPHOLSTERY

Vinyl upholstery is cold in winter and hot in summer, but it's durable and easy to care for. Leather upholstery is a luxury-car option, but the care for both kinds of upholstery is the same.

Vacuum the creases and crevices of your car's upholstery as part of your routine, general car care, but be especially careful not to scratch the upholstery with sharp-edged attachments or by exerting too much pressure. Use a whisk broom to remove loose soil or debris when you are unable to vacuum. Clean upholstery with a commercial product or a homemade solution. Use a leather or vinyl conditioner periodically to prevent cracking, drying out, and fading. When you use a commercial product, read and follow the manufacturer's instructions.

MAKE IT YOURSELF!

LEATHER OR VINYL UPHOLSTERY CLEANER

Make a warm, soapy solution using soap flakes and water. Apply the suds to the upholstery with a soft-bristled brush, working the cleaner gently into the grain. Wipe the upholstery clean with a damp sponge, and buff it dry with a soft cloth.

VINYL CAR TOPS

Some cars have decorative vinyl tops, which require special cleaning products to keep them looking good for a long time. Scrub the vinyl top with a soft-bristled brush and a mild cleaner to get soil out of the grain. Then apply a protective coating for vinyl to the car top to guard against damage from sun, pollutants, and extreme weather. Do not use ordinary car wax.

Many commercial products are available to clean and protect vinyl car tops. If you use one of these products, read and follow the manufacturer's instructions.

MAKE IT YOURSELF!

CLEANER FOR VINYL CAR TOPS CLEANER

Pour 1/8 cup dishwashing detergent into a pail, and add a hard stream of about 1 gallon warm water to make lots of suds. Apply the solution with a sponge and scrub with a brush. Rinse well, wipe dry, and apply a vinyl dressing for protection.

WINDOWS & WINDSHIELDS

Before self-service gas stations, shining car windows was one cleaning task that most people didn't do for themselves. But now that most of us pump our own gas, we also clean our own windshields, car windows, headlights, and taillights. Keeping them clear is essential to safe driving. Clean all exterior glass and plastic windows each time you refuel your car. Use a synthetic scouring pad to remove stubborn street grime and bugs. Make sure that the cloth with which you wipe the windows is free of grit that can scratch the surface. Ideally, you should use only a full-skin chamois; it will not streak and is unlikely to scratch your car windows.

Each time you wash the car, clean the glass and plastic windows inside and out with a glass-cleaning product or windshield-washer fluid. Clean the inside of the windows with strokes in one direction and the outside with strokes in another direction; this makes it easy to find and correct streaks.

To properly care for your windshield, always use specially formulated windshield-washer fluid. Keep the washer jets clear and adjusted so that they spray onto the windshield correctly. Replace windshield-wiper blades when they begin to smear or skip on the windshield. The blades will last longer if you always wet the windshield before using the wipers.

Mix ¼ cup vinegar in 1 gallon warm water. Wipe the windows inside and out with a cloth dipped in the solution. Then wipe with a clean, dry cloth. This solution also cleans plastic car windows.

YOUR GARAGE

* If you accidentally spill oil onto your garage floor, sprinkle salt on it and wait 15 minutes. The salt will soak up some of the liquid and make cleanup easier.

* To get rid of a motor oil spill on your concrete garage floor or driveway, mix 1 cup ammonia with a gallon of warm water. Dunk a stiff-bristled brush in the mixture, scrub away the spill, and then rinse with clear water.

* Another cleanup treatment for oil spills in the garage is to sprinkle on a mixture of baking soda and corn meal. Allow the mixture to soak in, then sweep or vacuum up.

* Baking soda can also remove tough stains from the garage floor. Sprinkle some on the spot, let stand, then scrub with a wet brush.

* To clean up oil, brake fluid, transmission fluid, and other spills on the garage floor, cover spot with clean cat litter. Allow it to absorb the liquid for at least an hour, then clean up.

* Freshen up a damp, musty garage with this simple remedy: Add 1/2 inch baking soda to the bottom of a paper grocery bag with handles; hang bag from the rafters. Change every 3 months.

* If you keep bumping into your garage wall with your car, hang a tennis ball from the ceiling at the exact spot where your windshield should be when you stop. When you bump the ball, you're home free.